The Christian Power Plan

David Ray

Word Books, Publisher

Waco, Texas

The Christian Power Plan

Scripture quotations from the Revised Standard Version of the Bible, copyrighted 1946, 1952, © 1971, 1973 by the Division of Christian Education of the National Council of the Churches of Christ in the U.S.A., and used by permission; Today's English Version of the New Testament, copyright © American Bible Society, 1966; *The Living Bible, Paraphrased* © 1962, 1965, 1966, 1967, 1968, 1970, 1971 by Tyndale House Publishers, Wheaton, Illinois, used by permission; *The New Testament in Modern English* by J. B. Phillips, © J. B. Phillips 1958, 1959, 1960, 1972; used by permission of The Macmillan Company.

Library of Congress catalog card number: 76–48537
ISBN 0–87680–476–8

Printed in the United States of America

With loving appreciation
to
a powerful and empowering staff that surrounds me
and to
the congregation of Central Presbyterian Church,
Jackson, Mississippi,
whom I have the pleasure of serving as minister.
They bless me!

Contents

Preface 9

1. He Who Expecteth Nothing Ain't Going
   to Be Deceived 11

2. The Assurance You've Always Wanted 24

3. Why Do People Suffer? 38

4. Beat Boredom 49

5. Discovering the Real You 61

6. The Security You've Been Searching For 73

7. Looking for Serenity? Here It Is! 85

8. Take Charge of Your Feelings
   and They'll Work for You 97

9. Get the Team Spirit
   and Do Away with Loneliness 109

10. Fill Up with Faith
    and Fade Out Your Fear 121

Notes 135

Preface

Increasingly, I feel a need for power extraordinary that touches and transforms life. In my experience with people, I have found that they too sense such a need and want answers that will help them tap the power. Those answers are not uncovered in pious ponderings, not even in position and prestige, but within. The power may result in prestige and position, but more importantly, it is power to face, accept, improve, and overcome. It is power that turns today into definite success. It is power that brings more meaning to events, suffering, old age, and death because it is power inside to confront events, suffering, old age, and death. It is power to act and react positively. It is power to shape and reshape things creatively. It is power willed by God. St. Paul wrote, "God has not given us a spirit of fear, but a spirit of *power* and love and a sound mind" (2 Tim. 1:7, Phillips, italics mine).

With that in mind, the purpose of this book is to outline the dynamics of power: how to gain it, grow it, accept it, increase it, maintain it, and use it. After hearing chapter titles, a friend said, "It looks like you're saying a life that really wins is within reach." Exactly! However, it requires a Christian power plan which reaches us where we are, as we are, and urges us forward to the persons we can become. I pray the content of this book propels you on to the power you have always wanted.

I am profoundly thankful to a new friend, Floyd W. Thatcher, vice-president and executive editor of Word Books, Publisher, for his positive and gentle way of helping me; to Mrs. Frances Fryant, Mrs. Anne Dalton, and Mrs. Pat Looney who have typed and retyped manuscripts; and to one of the world's most faithful and persistent encouragers, my wife, who would not let me quit.

More power to you,
David Ray

1. He Who Expecteth Nothing Ain't Going to Be Deceived

You will find amazing power if you develop a spiritual habit of positive expectation.

This chapter title is from the lyrics of a pop tune of another era, but as well as being catchy, the line describes one of the basic laws of life. What do you expect for yourself? of yourself? your husband? your wife? your children? your parents? your business associates? your neighbors? your job? your church? your life?

The power of expectation is enormous. What a person genuinely and deeply expects affects spiritual forces around him, his own attitude and actions, and the attitude and actions of others. For example, with fear and trembling, Linda assumed her new job as a secretary. "I don't expect to make it," she insisted. Linda thought, talked, and acted like she would fail, and the job lasted three months. Ed dreaded facing his neighbor about the three-hundred-dollar repair job needed on the fence which separated their property. When it was installed, they had agreed to share in keeping up the fence, but Ed said, "He's an old grouch, and I don't expect anything out of him." The neighbor lived up to what Ed expected.

Researchers at the University of Southern California re-emphasized that husband and wife tend to match the other's expectations. Sam expects Margie to be furious because he is late getting home from work and didn't call her. Margie expects him to look dimly on the new dress she bought on sale for eighty-eight dollars. John Wolcot, eighteenth-century satirist and poet, said, "Blessed are those who nought expect, For they shall not be disappointed." Sam and Margie weren't disappointed!

Children are most attuned to living up (or down) to what

is expected of them. Johnny is making F's in school. "Oh, you're a dummy," dad keeps telling him. "What else can we expect?" "A dummy I am," Johnny thinks, "and a dummy I'll be."

Frankie is making D in math. He begins to be tardy to class; he skips a few times. Eventually, Frankie's parents get a call from the principal. Mom and dad call Frankie in for a conference. "Son," they begin, "we don't expect you to be perfect, but we do expect you to do your best and we'll help you." Frankie concludes that they really care; he begins to understand the nature and spirit of what they expect. Before long, his math grade jumps to a high C.

The power of expectation is at work in every spiritual success. James put it clearly: "When you ask Him [God], be sure that you really expect Him to tell you" (James 1:6, LB).

John faced a huge, unexpected need. With a faith that meets such challenges head-on, John expected God to help him. He prayed like it, thought like it, talked like it, and acted like it. And God helped, for John met the conditions of divine involvement.

To a large degree, a life with power depends on your developing the spiritual habit of positive expectation, which, in essence, means that you condition yourself spiritually in such a way as to form the thought-habit of expecting a victorious outcome to your life on a day-by-day basis. What elements are required to achieve the spiritual habit of positive expectation?

Motivation

A man went out late one night to look for a lost friend. His search led him through a cemetery. The night was cold and foggy, and rain drizzled quietly in the dark. Unable to see where he was going, the man fell into an open grave.

It wasn't an in-place; so he did everything in his power to

get out, but the rain had made the sides slick and muddy. The harder he tried to get out, the worse the situation became. Finally, he thought, "Well, I'll have to wait until morning for somebody to help me out." Exhausted, the man sat down at one end of the grave, pulled his jacket tightly around him, and cuddled up to wait until morning.

A few minutes later another man came walking through the cemetery. He too couldn't see where he was going and fell into the same open grave. Like the first man, he tried with all his might to get out, but it seemed like an impossible task. Just as he was about to sit down and wait until morning, the man at the other end said, "It's no use. You can't get out." But he did! In one leap! He was motivated!

Motivation is that inner fire which stimulates a person to work toward his objective. It is the drive that keeps him going. Jesus was the most motivated person in history. With a cross before him, the Master still possessed inner fire. Stimulated by his Father's will, the inner drive grew, and he pushed on in pursuit of his divine objective.

Motivation is the difference between a two-cylinder and an eight-cylinder life. When God is at work in you, you are deeply motivated.

I know a man who was a three-time loser as a salesman. After being released from the third job, he began to ask himself some penetrating questions: Why am I here? What does it take? Who am I as I am? Who am I in terms of what I can become?

Those questions led him to a church where he heard about the love of a great God and the activity of God on his behalf. He accepted Christ into his life, and he began thinking and living a better way. The man discovered a fire burning within which created the will to be a credit to himself, his family, and society. Moreover, he wanted his life to reflect positively on God, his partner and friend. Basically, he found a motivation inside comparable to a nonstop mountain spring flowing with force and direction. On his fourth job, he became a perennial member of the life insurance industry's million-dollar round table.

Motivated persons have an unsinkable, sincere, winsome, contagious, enthusiastic force within. They are humans in divine hands, ignited, charged, and plussed. They become more concerned about getting a job done than who gets the credit. They realize it is just as easy to shoot at a bird on a limb thirty feet above the ground as it is to shoot at one on the ground the same distance away; therefore, they raise their sights.

I will always remember Mrs. Hayes, a seventy-eight-year-old woman I saw in the hospital. Her body was frail, and her face was wrinkled and thin, but she had a smile that drove away the tears. "Many people have given me up to die," she charged, "but I've got too much going to stop at the moment. There's a lot left for me to do, and I believe God is going to let me finish it." When I returned to the hospital a few days later, she had been released. Mrs. Hayes is one of the most motivated people I've met. As she told me about the force she felt within, her voice was lively and her eyes sparkled like diamonds.

How motivated are you? How strong is your motivation? Who is behind it? Let God motivate you.

Mental Ejection-Injection

Another element required to achieve the spiritual habit of positive expectation is what I refer to as the *mental ejection-injection process*. Everyone of us must master the art of ejecting defeating thoughts from our mental-stream.

A young man, only in his thirties, constantly thought he was dying, but he had a wife and four children. He said, "I can't leave these kids until they're grown and on their own." This simple determination kept him going. Although he was sure he was in the process of dying, he refused to die at that time. However, within a year after the last child moved away from home, he passed away. Doctors claimed there was no organic reason for his death. By habitual thought, he had grooved death into his personality to the extent that his body accepted and abode by it!

Faithfulness develops habit. Habit is the result of repetition. What you think on deeply, day in and day out, you will become. What you habitually think will, in some measure, tend to happen. That is one reason the apostle Paul advised: "Fix your thoughts on what is true and good and right. Think about things that are pure and lovely, and dwell on the fine, good things in others. Think about all you can praise God for and be glad about" (Phil. 4:8, LB).

After the Civil War, General Samuel Armstrong founded Hampton Institute for boys. Some of his students were from underprivileged backgrounds, and many had already programed their minds to defeat and destructive dependence. Realizing they needed to overcome such thinking to which environment and heritage had conditioned them, the general occasionally told the story of the woodchuck.

"Men," he would begin, "you all have heard of the woodchuck. Once there was a little woodchuck. Everyone knows that woodchucks can't climb trees, but, men, this woodchuck was being chased by a ferocious hound dog. Although he ran as fast as he could, the dog gained ground on him. The little woodchuck saw a tree and thought, 'Oh, if only I could get up that tree I'd be safe.' Just then, the big dog came around the corner and, men, the woodchuck climbed that tree!"

From this story, General Hampton commented that living is a matter of attempting what often seems impossible and that what a person does (or doesn't do) is proportionately affected by that which he thinks about the most.[1]

Failure thoughts need to be rudely, promptly, and unceremoniously booted out. Overcoming thoughts need to be warmly welcomed, entertained, and encouraged. "Let this mind [attitude] be in you, which was also in Christ Jesus" (Phil. 2:5). Your attitude is the prevailing tenor of your thoughts, the total of your most tenacious thinking.

Mental ejection-injection takes dedication, effort, and persistence. The following plan has helped many get started.

THIRTY-DAY MENTAL EJECTION-INJECTION PLAN

1. Release your life, as completely as you know and like you are, to Christ as much as you understand him.
2. Renew your commitment by coming to God often, especially when you are aware of something amiss in your life.
3. Read the Gospel of John and then Luke, for fifteen minutes each day, marking every reference to an act of God's love. Write to the side, "This means me."
4. Act and live the promises of Christ with enthusiasm, as best as you know.
5. Read the Epistle of 1 John once a week. It's short and powerful in reference to God's love and the power of that love in one's life.
6. Immerse yourself as much as possible with dedicated, positive, believing people. Their spirit will tend to rub off on you.
7. When you wake up every morning, first thing, affirm the love and presence of Christ. Use Psalm 118:24. Thank him for the night of rest, the day of opportunity, and thank him for the power of his Holy Spirit to guide you that day.
8. Pray regularly morning, noon, and night, even if only for a brief time.
9. Close the day with the Forgiver's Pledge: "Heavenly Father, I accept your forgiveness for every wrong in

my life this day. And I forgive everyone who has thought, spoken, and acted in a harmful way toward me this day."
10. Share your discoveries with at least one other person, or group.
11. At the very suggestion of a defeating thought, dismiss it from your mind with a positive Bible verse.

Respect Your Limitations

Humans are limited. For example, a friend of mine doesn't fully respect the limitations of his body because he goes at breakneck speed about fourteen hours a day for eight or nine days. Then his emotional apparatus tells him loud and clear that the body demands respect. He wakes up with fierce headaches, or develops stomach turmoil, or becomes so tense he cannot turn his neck without turning his whole body.

Respect insists that you: (1) Admit your limitations; (2) commit them to the Limitless One; and (3) submit them to positive uses.

Many famous people had more than the average limitations. Socrates, one of the brightest philosophers of all time, was an ugly man, not plain-looking, but actually ugly in appearance! When people saw him, they were unable to control themselves. Often they snickered and giggled in his presence. Yet Socrates's ready wit and rich wisdom drew an army of admirers.

Beethoven had a short frame, and his swarthy face was dotted freely with pock marks. At the peak of his career, the inimitable composer went totally deaf. Most experts consider his Ninth Symphony the crowning masterpiece from this creative genius, but the composer never heard one note of it.

Each year, millions of people thrill as they hear Handel's *Messiah* and its resounding "Hallelujah Chorus." That inspiring work is acknowledged by most authorities as the

greatest oratorio ever written. Huge in scale, sublime in concept, unfaltering in eloquence, it remains one of man's gran-
diose conceptions. At the time he wrote *Messiah,* Handel was
fifty-six years of age, pitifully poor, and suffering from
paralysis of the right side of his body.

In 1812, three-year-old Louis Braille was boring holes
through a heavy piece of leather in his father's harness shop.
Suddenly, an accident blinded young Louis for life. Fifteen
years later, at age eighteen, the young man invented a system
of reading for the blind which has brought help and hope to
millions of unsighted people.

Many consider St. Paul history's most prolific interpreter
of the Christian faith. There seems to be little doubt that the
world-wide spread of Christianity came from the impetus generated through Paul. His dedication, sacrifice, happiness,
optimism, love, faith, probing mind, expert salesmanship,
indomitable spirit, and tireless efforts speak for themselves.
Furthermore, Paul sincerely lived the way he fervently cham-
pioned. In other words, he practiced what he preached, but
Paul had a limitation.

As far as Bible scholars can determine, Paul suffered from
an acute and disfiguring form of ophthalmia, and he was
nearly blind. We don't know any more about it since Paul
didn't harp on his handicap. On several occasions, he asked
God to correct it, but the limitation remained. Paul discovered
two truths that will make each of us much better persons:
(1) God's delays are not God's denials; (2) accomplishments aren't prevented by limitations.

It is not always necessary to be free from limitations in
order to have a full and released life! An achiever can overcome his limitations! It is always necessary, however, to respect them and thereby capitalize on them. Paul was assured
that God's grace is sufficient, no matter what and how big
the limitation, and that divine power is stronger than any
human weakness.

I am thinking about Mercy Goodfaith who grew up in an orphanage in the great Midwest some years ago. Mercy was a hunchback, homely—in fact quite ugly in appearance. And she was frail. To add to these liabilities, she possessed a nasty disposition.

When Mercy was ten years old, a woman came to the orphanage and volunteered to adopt a girl. "But," she insisted, "I want a girl that no one else will take." One glance at Mercy and the woman exclaimed, "That's the girl! I'll take her!"

Over thirty years later, an investigator of institutions in another part of the country prepared his official report after inspecting a county orphanage. He wrote that the facilities were spotless and the children appeared to be remarkably happy. After supper, the girls and boys followed their matron into the living room where one girl played the organ and the other children sang with great enthusiasm.

Two of the children sat on each arm of the matron's chair and she cuddled the two smallest tots in her lap. At her feet, a boy took the hem of her dress and stroked it gently.

The investigator observed that the children worshiped the matron. And she obviously loved them very much. He closed his report by saying that she was a hunchback, homely in appearance, but her eyes sparkled like diamonds, giving her a certain beauty. Her name was Mercy Goodfaith.

It is not far-fetched to think that Miss Goodfaith developed as a beautiful, outgoing person because she learned to respect her limitations and capitalize on them.[2]

If you honestly respect your limitations, you will:

1. Discover that God's presence will sustain you.
2. Find out that divine power is stronger than any limitation you have.
3. Rid yourself of every limitation you can.
4. Use any limitation that remains to climb to a more meaningful life rather than as a club to barge your way through life.

5. Accept the limitation as a guideline to living instead of a stop sign.
6. Develop unusual resilience and strength because your keenest victory can be realized at the point where you overcome your biggest limitation.

Prayer

Not long before he died, Peter Wust, the European philosopher, was asked by some students for a final reflection on life. Dr. Wust said:

> The magic key is not reflection, as you might expect a philosopher to say, but prayer. Prayer as the most complete act of devotion makes us quiet and objective. . . . The greatest things in existence will only be given to those who pray.[3]

Robert Hall, nineteenth-century English clergyman, claimed that prayer serves as an edge and border to preserve the web of life from unraveling. And James Stalker wrote in *Imago Christi:*

> A wise man once said to me that he was too busy to be in a hurry. He meant that if he allowed himself to become hurried, he could not do all that he had to do. There is nothing like prayer for producing this calm self-possession.[4]

What is *prayer?* Honest communication with God, my friend. In prayer, a person, as and where he or she is, talks things over with God, as and where he is. Prayer is open conversation with God. It changes people, thoughts, attitudes, and events.

I remember the church member who told me how prayer had recently worked in the life of his family. The previous them like an avalanche. A family of ordinary means, they year had been the most difficult the family had ever encountered. Hospital bills and other unexpected expenses piled on reduced their budget to the barest level. But they did ask God for help and they believed that he would come to their aid. Even when conditions steadily became worse, they continued to ask and believe.

Just when they were at the end of their rope, a neighbor said, "My wife and I believe we ought to loan you six hundred dollars." That was a lot of money to the neighbors; they too were of average means. And that was a lot of money to my members.

No, the neighbor was not asked for the loan! There were no subtle hints. The explanation was, "We prayed and we began to feel that God wanted us to offer you this loan." There were no strings attached, just a request that the members repay the loan when they could.

A few days later, the neighbors who loaned the money received seven hundred dollars in the mail as repayment for another long-forgotten loan. They had not counted on those funds at all! After talking the sequence of events over, they said to my friends, "We got seven hundred dollars which we hadn't depended on. We've prayed about the loan to you and we believe we need to cancel it. OK?"

Consider the people, thoughts, attitudes, and events involved. A mistake? Perhaps a queer quirk of nature? "Oh," you may think, "it would have happened anyway." If you think so, read on.

Fulton Oursler, the bestselling author, shared this story in which he asked, "Was it a lucky break? Or was it the working out of the mystery contained in prayer?":

Dr. Herbert Booth Smith, a Presbyterian minister, stood on a ladder in his living room as he decorated a chandelier for Christmas. Suddenly, he heard a knocking overhead. He rushed upstairs to find his ten-year-old son, Bert, on the floor gasping. "Daddy, I can hardly get my breath!" While Mrs. Smith shook and massaged Bert, Dr. Smith raced to the telephone to call the doctor. He was out for the evening.

"Dear God," prayed the father, "let the next doctor be home." But he, too, was away. "Oh dear Lord," prayed Dr. Smith, "don't let my young boy die." He phoned another doctor. No answer. And another doctor. Still no answer. "Hurry," cried the mother upstairs. "For God's sake, hurry!"

Every doctor in town was away, but Dr. Smith remembered one in Hollywood, a number of miles from where he lived. Desperately, he phoned. "Bring your son to the phone," the doctor advised. "Tell me now, are the fingers curving into the palm? Are they turning blue? Is the skin a kind of sickly yellowish color?"

"Yes," Dr. Smith answered. "All of them!"

The doctor said, "Then undoubtedly he has edema or swelling of the larynx. He will have to have an emergency incision at once to save his life. I cannot possibly get there in time. Do everything you can to get a doctor!"

As he put down the receiver, Dr. Smith wondered why God would take his boy from him. As he dialed the hospital in the next town, the thought of death overwhelmed him. No one at the hospital could get in touch with a doctor near enough to be of help. He called another hospital in another town and he got the same reply.

Often, he had consoled parents who lost a young child, but now he was there himself! He phoned once more. The answer was the same. No one was close enough to help soon enough.

Carefully, he slipped the receiver back on the hook, sank to his knees, and prayed, "Heavenly Father, with all my heart and soul I entreat you to save the life of my little boy. But your will, not mine, be done. If my son must die, then thank you, dear Father, for the years we have had with him."

The phone rang.

It was the Hollywood doctor. "I've been frantically trying to get you, but your line has been busy. Thank God you got off! I've just learned there is a surgeon from overseas visiting in your city. He would know what to do."

Repeating the name and address over and over, the father sped to the doctor's house. Only minutes away from death, the boy was placed on the kitchen table and the doctor performed a tracheotomy whereby the windpipe was opened so that the lungs could get fresh air directly.[5]

Chance? The "way the cookie crumbled?" Never!

And to think that prayer will not help you develop that spiritual habit of positive expectation! Of course it will, because God will. But it requires the prayer-habit. The prayer-habit results in prayer-miracles. Daily prayer lessens daily cares.

Each day, especially at the beginning, talk to God. A regular time makes you prompt and punctual. Don't let feelings, conditions, and social and business demands interrupt you. Make whatever adjustments are needed. When you miss, pick up again without additional delay. Don't say, "Oh my, I missed it, so I'll forget it." That is defeating. Ask God to help you do it, and the results will amaze you. Prayer will become second nature to you, a natural and overcoming expression of life.

You'll develop the spiritual habit of positive expectation. Don't be surprised at the successes and achievements. You're using the power.

2. The Assurance
You've Always Wanted

You will grow a deep and dependable power if you practice positive assurances about life and death.

The overcomer has to be a tough-minded person these days. On a trip to a small town in Oklahoma, I had to fly in a commuter plane. If you've ever been on one, you are aware of their size. They are not as sturdy looking as the big 747's. That particular commuter appeared to have many years behind it, too many for me. I wasn't sure I wanted to get on board, but I had to fill my engagement.

When the pilot started the engine, I was positive I heard it miss a time or two. Still, we managed to get in position for take-off. "What do you think?" I whispered to the man across the aisle. He didn't say anything, but when I saw his fingers crossed, I suspected he had misgivings too!

Eventually we began moving down the runway. The plane coughed, bumped, and wobbled along. What little confidence I had was eroding. Belching and puffing billows of black smoke, the plane lifted into the air! Below, although not far enough below, I could see the Ozark mountains, splendidly outfitted in velvet green. Up ahead I saw a peak. Really it was an exaggerated hill, but to that aircraft, it might as well have been the Alps! "Lord," I prayed silently, "somebody has got to lift us over that mountain if we are going to make it. If this is your time for me to come home, I'll accept it. But if it's all the same to you, I'd just as soon honor my appointment in Oklahoma."

Bobbing and weaving its way through, the plane landed safely at our destination with eleven sick passengers, including me. I am certain fear had as much to do with the sickness as the bobbing and weaving and sudden ups and downs. But the airsickness didn't begin to match our gratefulness as that plane finally shimmied to a stop!

International challenges also tell us we need workable assurances. Complaining of nagging headaches, nervousness, and fear, a patient listened to the doctor advise, "What you really need is a few months' vacation on the moon." You may feel like that at times, especially when you hear a physicist say:

> If three certain words are ever spoken into a certain telephone at Strategic Air Command Headquarters, hundreds of bombers will take to the sky, carrying multi-megaton nuclear bombs to the enemy. In a number of hours, claims the S.A.C., 50 million Russians will be killed. And when the tumult subsides this planet of ours will be an irrevocable inferno of radioactive debris.

A congressional committee estimated that an attack on the United States could easily kill twenty-five million of us and leave another thirty million injured so badly that death would result. It is not difficult to believe the Nobel Prize winner who stated that science has created a world in which Christianity is a necessity.

Dr. George Wald, also a Nobel Prize winner and professor of biology at Harvard University, shakes out of us every ounce of complacency remaining when he says, "The only way the world is going to stop short of the brink of nuclear holocaust is a return to God and the principles of the Bible. That is what the young people are trying to tell us."

Speaking for a scientific symposium at Colorado State University, Dr. Wald received a tremendous ovation after he said, "Nuclear holocaust can only be averted by faith, love, and hope and the precious principles of the Bible. I know that this is the sheerest nonacademic sentimentality but I'm convinced that this is the only way we are going to prevent total chaos."

Dr. Wald demonstrated some bright thinking. Certainly he points out the need for assurance which is helpful for living in today's world. What assurances will add life to your day?

Life can become worthwhile. Someone asked, "Where does the Bible say it is wrong to take your life? A friend who is subject to severe depression asked me this the other day, and I want to know what to answer." One of the Ten Commandments is "Thou shalt not kill." Self-destruction is killing. The body is the temple of God. It is not ours to mutilate, desecrate, or annihilate. Furthermore, Jesus' life was a masterful affirmation of life. Even his death expressed life. Death, to him, was a gateway to life forevermore! Hear him declare life-affirming promises: "The Son of Man is not come to destroy men's lives, but to save them" (Luke 9:56). "I am come that they might have abundant life" (John 10:10). About Jesus it was written, "In him was life; and the life was the light of men" (John 1:4). The central theme of these verses is: Your life may be worthwhile.

You are mistaken if you think other people are destined for heights while you are doomed to hopelessness. "God is ready to give blessings to all who come to him" (Luke 4:19, LB). If your life is not worthwhile, it may be. If you are not happy, you may be. Happiness is for you too. You need not stay like you are.

Your life as it is this moment may not be worth living. That depends on what your life is. Substance makes the difference. But if it is not worth living now, it is not worth ending either.

Anyone who is not prepared for living is not ready for dying. Anyone who is fully alive doesn't want to push death. You can count on this: Your life is worth changing, and thereby it becomes worthwhile. You may not be perfectible. No human is! But you are improvable. The efforts and results will make the difference.

Life can be an overcoming experience. When asked to autograph books, I offer a silent prayer that something will be given me to write which is meaningful, especially to the person receiving the book. Often I write, "Life may be overwhelming or overcoming."

I got a telephone call one Saturday night about eight o'clock. "My name is Mr.——," he said. "I come to your church once in awhile. Now, I know it's Saturday night, but I simply must see you."

We agreed to meet at my office in thirty minutes. When they came in, I greeted Mrs.—— and reached out my hand to shake his. The man withdrew it, put his hand behind him, and with head lowered said, "I won't shake hands with you. After you find out what's happened, you will not want to shake my hand."

The smartly dressed couple sat down, but he would not look at me. "I can't even hold my head up," he cried. "I'm so ashamed. My life is trash. I'm whipped."

With forty years of married life behind him and an unblemished career as a professional man, he had been accused of a serious immoral act. "Oh, I am dirt cheap," he said. "I've always had the most disgusting feeling when I read about such things in the paper. 'They're not worth shooting,' I'd think of the offenders. Now me! They tell me I did it when I was drunk. I asked my wife to take our gun and shoot me. I didn't have the courage to do it myself."

Fortunately, she didn't. She tried to be understanding. Obviously, he was at the end of his rope, and he felt overwhelmed. We talked, and I read from the Bible. Before they left, I asked for his hand. As tears rushed down his distress-stricken face, he said, "Are you sure you want it?"

"I'm sure." And I took hers as we formed a triangle of prayer.

It is possible for life to be *overcoming*. He was overwhelmed then. Since that fateful event, he has become overcoming. In fact, today he is an enthusiastic Christian, a member of the church, a warm, personal friend, and an extraordinary example.

What has you down? Whatever it is, it has you spoofed. You can rise up and overcome!

God will guide you. Divine guidance is a tremendous experience. People complain of a drab, dull existence. Their days are blurred without the concise shape given by a sense of divine appointment. Guidance can and will change all that! Everybody needs somebody bigger than he or she is to lend direction to life!

What is the secret to this direction? "Trust the Lord completely; . . . In everything you do, put God first, and he will direct you and crown your efforts with success" (Prov. 3:5–6, LB). This releases you from a humdrum existence, for you feel the higher pull of life. Your day has more punch to it, for a force bigger than yourself is behind, beside, and before you all the way. "If any of you lacks wisdom, he should pray to God, who will give it to him; for God gives generously and graciously to all" (James 1:5, TEV). Here is how to experience guidance:

1. *Ask* God for it. (This is for your benefit, not his!)
2. *Open* yourself for it. (Trust God completely for direction! Put him first in your life!)
3. *Listen* from within. (Don't expect sounds from the woodwork or a strange voice out of the sky! So often we rush. "God, please this, that and the other," we say. "Got to go, God." And we zip up our heart and mind and we are off to other matters.)
4. *Take* the direction you believe is right. (God will lead you and crown your life with success!)
5. *Act* on it. (Divine guidance always leads to seeable results! It is practical!)

God's guidance reinforces resources (you have what it takes, whatever "it" is); increases accuracy (greater amount of right decisions); decreases strain (wear and tear on the body, mind, and spirit); and sharpens efficiency (get more from what you put in). Divine guidance frees the higher power for your life. There is more than you alone; therefore, you will surprise yourself at what can be done!

Think victory thoughts. Victory thinking is a fundamental prerequisite to success. Defeat thoughts pave the road to failure.

A study of tramps showed that they scored as high on intelligence tests as any other representative group of men of their age. However, they differed considerably in their mental and emotional characteristics. They were apt to be passive, submissive, depressed, and resigned to feelings of helplessness and inferiority. These characteristics relate to thinking.

Victory thoughts coat your mind with strength, conquest, and achievement. These thoughts rely on faith and visualization. "When you pray and ask for something, believe that you have received it, and everything will be given whatever you ask for" (Mark 11:24, TEV). That is amazing! It answers the charge of unanswered prayers.

Ask for something. Don't ramble! Be definite! Believe (which is faith) that you *have* received it. How is it possible to do that unless you picture in your mind what you are receiving? After you ask, gently close your eyes. Don't press or tighten them. Visualize yourself receiving that for which you have asked in faith. Spiritual and mental forces combine for tremendous results.

Dr. Cecil Osborne points out such amazing results in his best-selling book, *The Art of Understanding Yourself*. The church Dr. Osborne pastored has sponsored many mission congregations. As one subdivision rapidly developed, he talked with the builder about a site for another church, but the contractor said he wasn't interested in churches and did not intend to provide a site for one.

A few weeks later, Dr. Osborne drove through the area again. The hundreds of new families moving in ignited a more determined fire in his heart to see a congregation in that area. "Lord," he prayed, "if you want a church here, you can show us the way to accomplish it. Meanwhile, I'll turn it over to you."

The next day, he shared his dream with a friend who was well acquainted with real estate. Dr. Osborne asked him to see what he could do about a site. Later in the week, the man reported that he found a small pie-shaped piece of land the developer would sell, but it was too small for a church. However, he discovered that property adjacent to the pie-shaped parcel was owned privately. The owner bought it before the developer purchased surrounding land. The two pieces put together would be enough for the new church.

An offer was made on the two parcels of land, and it was accepted. One thousand dollars was paid as a deposit, and another twelve thousand dollars was needed within ninety days. During lunch with another friend, Dr. Osborne mentioned his dream for a church in the subdivision. "Five years ago," he stated, "we could have bought the land for five thousand dollars. Now, they want twelve thousand, and the way prices are climbing, it will be twenty-five thousand before long." The man listened with interest.

In reply, he said, "I'm selling a piece of land in less than ninety days. I give 30 percent of my income to God; 30 percent of my profit on this sale will be slightly more than twelve thousand dollars. I'll send you a check when the sale is completed."

Not aware that his friend would have twelve thousand dollars to give or that he would want to give it, Dr. Osborne found himself talking at the right time to the right person who had the means and the inclination to meet a need.[1] How did this come about?

Dr. Osborne claims that he put the idea on a mental screen, visualized it, and let God help him realize it. That is the secret of victory in any undertaking: faith and visualization.

Flash your dream on the screen of your mind, often, every day, again and again! Visualize it as taking place! Let God help you realize it!

This plan applies to every area of life—worship, work, play, family, and so on. A great fisherman used victory thinking. On many occasions, he would be in the same boat as others and catch catfish after catfish while his friends, using the same gear and bait, cast in the same spot and caught nothing. When asked about it, he answered, "I put the old 'squeeza-ma-jintum' on them. Mentally, I get down where they are, and I tell them to bite the bait. I see them snapping at the hook. I believe it will work. That's all I can tell you about it."

Nothing is impossible when you follow the plan of victory thoughts. Believe it! By habitually thinking victory, you meet certain inner conditions required for lasting happiness.

Think big. David Schwartz tells about a sales meeting at which the marketing director had the leading company salesman on the platform. He was a common-looking sort of a fellow who had earned fifty thousand dollars the past year. Other salesmen had averaged ten thousand.

The boss said, "I want you to take a good look at Harry. See 'im? Now what's Harry got that the rest of you haven't? Harry earned five times the average, but is Harry five times smarter? No, not according to I.Q. tests. I checked and they show Harry about average in that department.

"Did Harry have a better territory than the rest of you?

"No, his accounts averaged about the same.

"Did Harry have more education? No! Better health? No!

"Then maybe he worked five times longer than you men? Sorry, he didn't.

"In fact, he took more time off than most of you!

"Harry's about as average as an average guy could be except for one thing. The difference between Harry and the rest of you is that Harry thought five times bigger. The size of your thinking makes the difference." [2]

You may feel that thinking big violates humility. On the contrary, humility is not the art of thinking little of yourself. Such thinking is but the mirror of your view of God. Humility is not the philosophy or theology of "what a worm am I." Humility is thinking *honestly* of yourself.

The Bible says, "Be honest in your estimate of yourselves, measuring your value by how much faith God has given you" (Rom. 12:3, LB). The trouble is, we get to thinking of ourselves as we're not. A teenager heard dad talk about his part in World War II. From the sound of things, you'd think the Allies were a one-man gang. Finally, the son asked, "Dad, did anyone help you win the war?"

A humble person will not be put down nor will he be humiliated. As James Russell Lowell, the nineteenth-century poet-essayist, put it, "Humbleness is always grace, always dignity." Humility includes personal pride and self-respect. In the words of E. H. Chapin, nineteenth-century American clergyman, "Though we may be servants of all, we should be servile to none."

Humility is thinking *hopefully* of yourself. Think what you can become when your life is in Christ's hands. You are wondrously made, and you can do all things through Christ who strengthens you. As Phillips Brooks, the nineteenth-century American bishop, put it, "The true way to be humble is *not to stoop* until you are smaller than yourself, but to *stand* at your real height against some higher nature that will show you what the real smallness of your greatness is." [3] Do this and you will find yourself thinking big.

Believe. There is more power in believing than you can possibly dream. A young ministerial student went to the Holy Land on the strength of believing. When he heard that his pastor planned to go, he went to him and asked how much it cost and would the minister mind if he went along. The pastor replied that it cost thirteen hundred dollars, assured him that he would be glad to have him along, and inquired as to which rich uncle had passed on and left him a bundle! The minister knew the young man was paying all his expenses through divinity school and that his parents did not have thirteen hundred dollars to spare. There was no rich uncle! There was no other windfall! As a matter of fact, the young man had no visible means of support!

"But," he said to the pastor, "don't you believe it would be good for me to go to the Holy Land? Wouldn't it enrich my theological studies? Wouldn't it help make me a better minister to have firsthand, on-site, eye-and-hand contact with the places where our Lord ministered?"

His pastor agreed.

"Then," continued the young man persistently, "let's pray about it."

In two weeks, the student told the minister that he had definitely arrived at the point where he believed God wouldn't be offended if he went to the Holy Land. "So, count on me going," he said. "I *believe God* will make it possible."

His minister let him know they'd have to remit the money in four weeks. "Have you any known leads?" questioned the inquisitive pastor.

"Not at this time," replied the young man, "but I want to go in the worse way. I am convinced it's the thing to do, and I *believe God* will open the door."

In two weeks, the young man reported he didn't have the thirteen hundred dollars yet, but God is good. In three weeks, he reported that he didn't have the funds in hand at the moment, however, God still had seven days in which to work, and he *believed God* could do it. Four days before due day, the minister visited a man and his wife who loved Christ and the church and were intensely interested in the development of young seminarians. God had blessed them with more than the basic necessities of life, and they were generous with their gifts to God's work.

Before leaving, the minister felt constrained to tell them the story of the young man. "Seldom," he said, "have I seen such dogged faith in one person."

"We'd like to see him have the experience of going to the Holy Land with you," they said. "We'd like to sponsor him!"

Believing is the essential ingredient common to success in anything worthwhile! It opens doors and overcomes mountains. It attracts people and conditions required to achieve the objective. It repels defeat, withstands assaults, and adjusts and revises where necessary.

A believing person is the most powerful person on earth. He or she possesses spiritual dynamite. What makes the difference? Faith in the Lord. Success doesn't require perfect faith but complete faith in a perfect Lord. It doesn't take a big faith but faith in the great God who can.

There is foreverness to you. Time-consciousness is so ingrained into the human system that limitless time boggles the mind. Set the alarm. Get up. Eat at 7 A.M. Leave at 7:30. Arrive at work at 8 A.M. Lunch at noon. Supper at 6 P.M. Bed at 11:00. Time-consciousness also applies to church. Sunday school at 9:30. Worship at 11:00. Out at 12:00. Hopefully!

Although as humans we are conscious of time, we yearn for ongoing life. Someone told me about a man who has spent thirty thousand dollars to have his body frozen after he dies. He hopes some day science will be able to thaw him out, repair his body, and allow him to live again. One time, a famous actress hosted one hundred movie stars at a come-as-you-were party; the guests dressed as the persons they believed they were in previous lives. There seems to be something inside us that leaps out after everlastingness. In the third act of *Our Town* by Thornton Wilder, the stage manager says, "We all know that *something* is eternal. And it ain't houses, and it ain't names, and it ain't earth, and it ain't even the stars . . . everybody knows in their bones that *something* is eternal, and that something has to do with human beings." But real ongoing life was the theme of Jesus' pronouncement to Martha long ago. "I am the resurrection and the life; he who believes in me . . . shall never die" (John 11:25, RSV).

In the flow of foreverness, death becomes a doorway to the Lord, by faith in the Lord. Peter Marshall used to preach a great message entitled "Go Down Death." In it he told of a boy who had a terminal disease. When the lad fully realized he would die, he asked, "Mommy, what's it like to die?"

Mom hurried to the kitchen to stir some soup—and wipe away her tears. She gripped the edge of the kitchen counter and pressed so hard that her knuckles turned white. "O God," she prayed, "give me the words to say." She felt a fresh illumination coming out of the depths of her soul.

"Kenny," she said when she returned to his room, "you remember when you were a tiny boy, how you'd play so hard that when evening came you would be too tired to undress? You'd just tumble into mother's bed and fall asleep. But that wasn't your bed. You belonged somewhere else. And in the morning, you'd wake up in your own bed, in your own room. Dad carried you there. Remember? Well, sweetheart, death is like that. We wake up some morning and find ourselves in the other room—the room that is best ours and where we best belong—because Jesus loves us."

Yes, there is a foreverness to you! You may prepare for it now! Your faith in the Lord will drain away at least some of the apprehension which surrounds death.

Death is an event of God's love. Sir Oliver Lodge, the English physicist and author, said death is "an inevitable adventure." Herman Hooker, nineteenth-century Episcopal minister and author: "We die that we may die no more." Francis Bacon: "It is as natural for a man to die as to be born." Dr. Leslie Weatherhead's illustration of an embryo is one of the most forceful I've ever read.[4] The little one is snug under mother's heart, but the time arrives to be born into this world. "No," demands the embryo, "I don't want to leave this place. I'm secure. My needs are all met here. It's warm, and I'm safe. I'm happy and satisfied; I feel love where I am. To be born is to die. I don't want to die by being born. Stop! Stop! Stop the process! Please don't! Oh, God stop it!"

A child is born. He feels the love and care of parents. He rollicks and plays and laughs. He grows into teens, learns more about himself, others, and the world. He becomes a man. Hardships, buffetings, and disappointments are mixed with joys and happiness. Middle age, life is good. Senior years, his hair turns gray; he becomes a bit feeble. He has to adjust from teen and middle years to the sixties. He knows he has to die. "But," he insists, "I don't want to die. I like it here. The beauty, the mountains, the forests, my family, my friends, the rhythmic ocean, the sandy shores, the touch of rain, the warm sunshine. I like it! I like it! I don't want to leave this place. To die is to become dead. I don't want to become dead. Stop! Stop! Stop the process! Oh, God, stop it!"

Use your faith. For one moment, do you believe, or is it legitimate for you to believe, that the God who brought him from his mother's womb into this world and who accepted him as his redeemed child has any other design than one of love by taking him from this human world to God? Then, as an event of God's love, death is the entry to new life eternal just as birth is the entry to new life mortal. Norman Macleod writes:

We picture death as coming to destroy; let us rather picture Christ as coming to save. We think of death as ending; let us rather think of life as beginning, and that more abundantly. We think of losing; let us think of gaining. We think of parting; let us think of meeting. We think of going away; let us think of arriving. And as the voice of death whispers, "You must go from earth," let us hear the voice of Christ saying, "You are but coming to Me." [5]

Down with fear; up with faith! Down with setback; up with a step forward! Down with tomb-doom; up with triumph! The Bible assures, "And the ransomed of the Lord shall return, and come to Zion with singing; everlasting joy shall be upon their heads; they shall obtain joy and gladness, and sorrow and sighing shall flee away" (Isa. 51:11, rsv). Sunset . . . sunrise. No more tears or sorrow or pain. No more dying, or sin or night. Light, love, liberty, life! Unending, unspotted, unspoiled. Defeat? Hardly! "O death, where is thy sting? O grave where is thy victory? . . . Thanks be to God, which giveth us the victory through our Lord Jesus Christ" (1 Cor. 15:55, 57, kjv).

I had a profound experience at the bedside of a young man dying of cancer. Moments before he passed on, he turned his eyes toward mine and squeezed my hand tightly. "Listen," he said, "I hear music! Beautiful music! Chimes, strings, organ, choir!" Like mine, Handel's *Messiah* was among his favorites, especially the "Hallelujah Chorus." "Do you hear it?" he asked. "Do you hear the music? I'm going home where the music is." No, I didn't hear it, but I believe he did. For him, death was an event of God's love.

Tough-minded assurances are just what life orders for tough times. Use them! Live them! And you'll become an unaverage person because you have unlocked power extraordinary.

3. Why Do People Suffer?

You will increase your power if you accept a more adequate understanding of suffering.

The woman was flat on her back as I talked with her. She looked intently at the ceiling. Even the slightest movement exacerbated suffering of the most excruciating sort. As she talked, tears began to flood her eyes and trickle down the sides of her face. "This is the sixth time for me to be laid up in seven years," she said. "If it's not one thing, it's another." A series of accidents had left the woman with a great deal of mental and physical pain. "I've thought about ending it all," she continued. "Had it not been for the church, I probably would have killed myself. Why do I suffer? Why does anyone suffer?"

This was one of the biggest questions I'd ever been asked. It became the catalyst for a period of serious study, evaluation, and research on my part. I arrived at seven answers. There may be more, but there are at least seven.

Attention's Sake

For some people suffering is an ego factor, perhaps an unconscious one. A sure fact reemphasized by child psychologists is that children's behavior often reflects their desire for attention. The little girl chatters endlessly in an attempt to attract mother's attention, and she gets it. Mother yells at her to be quiet! The little boy manages to create all kinds of perplexing circumstances, often in a search for attention. He deserves it at both ends—the heart and bottom!

A mother of six received a playpen from friends when the new baby arrived. "Thank you very much for the pen," she wrote. "Thank you! Thank you! Thank you! It's wonderful.

Every afternoon I sit in it and read and the children can't get near me!"

Grown-ups aren't necessarily adults. The disciples of Jesus long ago proved that when they got into an argument as to who was the greatest. We too employ childish techniques to let people know we're around. Emotionally, we bang our spoons on the table and cry.

A businessman developed terrible headaches. His wife began to wait on him hand and foot, and his system found this a welcome change. Long after he had overcome the physiological ailment, he was still having headaches. Later he admitted it had become an ego problem. A young man unable to walk discovered the attention heaped on him satisfying. He had previously starved for attention. Six months after his physical condition had been corrected, he was still confined to a wheelchair. An emotionally handicapped woman went through an extended period of therapy. During that time, others did her housework. As far as science was concerned, she was well, but when asked to do even routine chores, she replied, "I can't. I'm not up to it."

Such persons have a sufferer's complex. "Ah, ha," they tell themselves in one way or another, "I get what I want by hurting." Their system then concludes that pain is worth it in order to achieve the objective—attention.

A Choice

The Bible says Moses chose to suffer with the people of God rather than enjoy the fleeting pleasures of sin (see Heb. 11:25). Choice is setting the mind. In *Prayer Is the Mightiest Force in the World,* Frank Laubach wrote that the future is menaced by small minds. So is the present. So is life. Dr. Laubach said, "Every thought tends to become true in proportion as it is intense and as it is long dwelt upon." [1]

What we do is set in motion by what we think. History is

made by what people do; yet thought (or the lack of it) is behind action. Dr. David Martin of the University of Southern California was correct when he said, "You are not what you think you are. What you think, you are." [2]

It is not uncommon for people to think themselves into suffering. They choose to suffer, but unlike Moses their suffering is destructive rather than constructive. However, it is nonetheless real. It hurts. It is painful. But it is the product of un-Christlike thinking.

Violating Laws of Health

Since our bodies are gifts from God, they deserve the finest treatment we can give them. We need to take the Bible seriously when it says our bodies are the temple of God (1 Cor. 3:16), dwellings of the Lord. Precious laws govern health: sleep (without sufficient sleep, you destroy your body and mind); relaxation (without relaxing, you build up tensions which can erode the strongest person); recreation (re-create through diversification, that is, take time to build up body and mind through activities different from your normal routine). Seldom do I drive to my office the same route on two consecutive days because I know it is necessary to break normal routine. There is a long-tested and well-proven equation for those who consistently, habitually violate the laws of health: Hurry equals bury!

A friend of mine began a sheet metal company when he was a young man. Mike was serious about the business and a super go-getter. As the company grew, he needed to delegate authority and responsibility, but in his heart Mike felt that "if you want a job done right, you've got to do it yourself."

He found himself working seven days a week, fifteen hours a day at a breakneck pace. Even when his body was not involved in business, his mind was. The mental motor ran continuously. He interfered with the pattern given by the

Lord: rest, relaxation, and recreation. The inevitable day arrived when Mike could not rest even for a brief time. Within a minute or two after lying down, he would jump up. Of course, his mental as well as his physical system was affected, and he had to be hospitalized for several weeks.

Violating Laws of God

A bedraggled man walked into my office some time ago. His face was drawn, and his body bore the marks of a man who had fought his way through life. "I no want to fight no more," said this native of Jamaica. "I want peace. I want to live in peace." He pulled out of his pocket the only article he owned other than the ragged clothes and well-worn shoes he had on. I unfolded it and read. It was a dismission certificate from the Ohio State Penitentiary. He had spent twenty-two years of his life in that institution.

"Mr.——" I asked, "how did you get there?"

"At sixteen," he explained, "I was told I killed two policemen. I no remember doing it, but the evidence show I did. I was kept in juvenile hall until I was eighteen, then moved to death row. Out of the twenty-two years in prison, I spent fifteen on death row." Not knowing what to do (he hadn't learned a skill in prison) or where to go (he had no known living relatives), he came to me for advice.

This man's suffering was caused by a violation of God's laws. Basically, those laws, including the Ten Commandments, pertain to every generation. In thinking about the pertinence of the commandments at every age, James Russell Lowell wrote:

> In vain we call old notions fudge;
> And bend our conscience to our dealing;
> The Ten Commandments will not budge,
> And stealing will continue stealing.[3]

When you get down to it, a person does not really break those laws. He breaks himself over them and suffers!

For Others

People also suffer for others. Jesus Christ suffered and died for others. St. Paul suffered for the Corinthian Christians. "It is all for your sake" (2 Cor. 4:15, RSV).

Some time ago, I heard about a man in Florida who operated one of those drawbridges over a river. His job was to lift the bridge and let the ships go through, then lower it back into place for the trains to cross over. One day, a ship blew its horn, signaling him to lift the bridge. There were only twelve minutes before a large passenger train was due with hundreds of people on it. The train was speeding at one hundred miles per hour, and there was no way to flag it down. After the boat had gone under the bridge, the operator started to press the button to lower it. Suddenly, he noticed his five-year-old son sitting on one of the gigantic cogs that raised and lowered the bridge. He looked at his watch and saw that in two minutes the train would dash across the bridge. There was not time to get his son off and lower the bridge. With a bitter cry, the man turned his head and pushed the button for the bridge to be lowered. It barely got down in time for the train to pass. Afterward, the man ran to where his son was and found him ground to pieces; he was beyond recognition, every bone crushed. The decision was painful: Save his son and let three hundred people plunge into the river, or let his son die and save three hundred passengers. He chose the latter. By so doing, he suffered for others.

In *Man's Search for Meaning* Dr. Viktor Frankl advised patients that the suffering they go through is God's way of sparing others that suffering. The loss of a loved one first spares the mate of suffering for you. The loss of a job spares someone else suffering the loss of his job. This, claims the noted counselor, is suffering for others.[4]

Because of Others

Thousands of innocent children were victims of the war in Indo-China. They and others suffered and are suffering in a way that breaks the hearts of sensitive people around the world. Nothing they did brought on the war. They have no political ambitions. At this point communism or freedom is irrelevant to them. They haven't devised any cruel, inhumane plans of destruction. They haven't plotted to overthrow any government. They haven't violated any peace agreements. Yet they suffer. Why? Because of others.

Since 1970, researchers have pointed out that the children of alcoholic mothers or drug addicts may be born as alcoholics or drug addicts. The Bible calls this visiting the sins of the parents on children. The little ones directly and of their own accord consume neither a drop of alcohol nor a cubic centimeter of narcotics; yet they suffer.

A rumor can cause suffering because of others. So can a lie. A public figure was accused of gross wrongdoing. Newspapers blazed the story on the front page. People were inflamed. "I knew it," they said. "Crooked just like other politicians." On the second day, a follow-up story was printed in a less conspicuous place, but this one began to moderate the charges. On the third day, another story, hidden somewhere in the middle of the paper, all but vindicated the man. As it turned out, this devoted official and faithful Christian was innocent. The allegations had been made by envious competitors; however, the damage was done. A reputation had been tarnished.

Life Includes Some Suffering for Everyone

But what about an infant deformed from birth? A child ravaged by polio? A boy crippled for life by muscular dystrophy? Victims of hurricanes, earthquakes, and other unexplainable acts of nature? Life is far from a cloudless journey. Each one goes through some fire. The difference is kind and intensity. What can you do?

Take inventory of yourself. Honestly examine yourself, God as your helper, and begin to make needed changes in your life.

It is unlikely that you will make any substantial change unless you are motivated by suffering or pain of some kind. In *The Art of Counseling,* Dr. Rollo May said, "People then should rejoice in suffering, strange as it sounds, for this is a sign of the availability of energy to transform their character . . . to the nonegocentric person every moment of suffering is the opportunity for growth." [5] Unlike what he bestowed on the animals, God has blessed you with a remarkable freedom to change. You may think that environmental, social, circumstantial, or physical conditions lead you like a lamb to the slaughter. However, the kind of person you become, even through suffering, is essentially the result of a decision you make! In order to make the right decision, take inventory, but don't be overly critical of yourself. And don't dwell excessively on your shortcomings.

By the power of Jesus Christ received into your life now, determine to gain victory through suffering. Don't let it win! Don't be victimized by it!

George Matheson has been an inspiration to millions of people for a long time, mainly because he would not let suffering victimize him. As George entered a promising career, a doctor said, "George, you'd better see your friends. Before long, darkness will settle upon you and you'll see them no more." That was his way of saying George was going totally blind and soon.

Matheson was engaged to a lovely young woman, his sweetheart, the apple of his eye. He told her the doctor's prognosis and that in all honesty he felt he must give her a chance to back out of their engagement.

She terminated the relationship. The pain that engulfed young Matheson was great; yet he did not allow it to overwhelm him. In fact, during that time—when he was losing his sight and had lost his fiancée—Matheson wrote the hymn "O Love That Wilt Not Let Me Go."

> O Love that wilt not let me go,
> I rest my weary soul in thee;
> I give thee back the life I owe,
> That in thine ocean depths its flow
> May richer, fuller be.
>
> O Joy that seekest me through pain,
> I cannot close my heart to thee;
> I trace the rainbow through the rain,
> And feel the promise is not vain
> That morn shall tearless be.[6]

One of Britain's most dynamic ministers, Dr. Leslie Weatherhead, dedicated his book *Why Do Men Suffer?* to his mother and sister, two victors *over* and not victims *of* suffering.

> Dedicated in unfailing remembrance to Elizabeth Mary Weatherhead, my mother, and Muriel Weatherhead, my sister, whose bodies were defeated in the battle of painful disease, but who wrested from that defeat a spiritual victory which challenged and inspired all who knew them, and made glad the heart of God.[7]

You are not fully conditioned to a certain, irrevocable outcome before which you are powerless! As Dr. Viktor Frankl states, "Man does not simply exist, but always decides what his existence will be, what he will become in the next moment." [8]

Pray through your suffering. James advised, "Is anyone among you suffering? Let him pray" (James 5:13, RSV).

Pray affirmingly. To *affirm* means to confirm, to ratify, it is the opposite of deny. Affirm Christ's love, power, and stamina as yours today. Affirm Christ's nearness, where you are, now! You say, "I do not feel God's presence," or, "I feel he is far removed from me." Remember, faith is bigger and greater than feeling. Feeling can mislead you. Affirm anyway —with or without feeling.

Pray positively. The human tendency while suffering is to pray negatively. *Can't, won't* and *don't* are the usual words used, but the need is to pray positively. Use "God can, God will, God does, therefore and thereby, I can, I will, I do." Look on the greatness and bigness of Christ. Read, or have someone read to you, his acts of greatness in Matthew, Mark, Luke, and John. Think about them. Meditate on him. Picture him doing them. Then begin to pray in that spirit.

Pray thankfully. Once I saw a bumper sticker which read, "Attitude Is Contagious . . . Is Yours Worth Catching?" An attitude of gratitude will do wonders for you; so mention often that for which you are, or can be, thankful. It begins to affect your attitude and upgrade it. In addition, it affects your activity. Thanksgiving translates into thanks-living!

Through honest prayer, you assume more and more the strength of God for suffering. You gain more and more the wisdom of God and the winner's attitude of God toward suffering. Try it!

Accept suffering as a means and not an end. Remember, you do not need a life without suffering. Rather, you need a life that has enough meaning to it that even through suffering you advance.

The cocoon of the emperor moth is shaped like a flask. To develop fully, it must force its way through the narrow neck of the cocoon, a process that takes hours of intense struggle. Entomologists explain that the pressure to which the moth is subjected is nature's way of forcing a life-giving substance into the creature's wings.

Suppose you wanted to lessen the suffering of the moth; so you took some small scissors and snipped the tiny threads at the neck of the cocoon. That would release the cocoon and make it larger at that point. Then the moth's emergence would be both effortless and painless, but the creature would never develop those rainbow-colored wings by which it could gracefully fly through the air. Instead, it would spend a few hours of life crawling around on the ground in a dazed, confused state. By making its emergence effortless and painless, you would have made it impossible for the life-giving substance to be forced into its wings.

You're neither an insect nor a creature. You're a *person* for whom God cares very much. Suffering must be accepted as a *means* and not the end! If it's allowed to be the end, it has defeated you.

Set your attention on the higher plane. There is more to your life than suffering. You are much more than the sum total of biological, psychological, and sociological situations. You are much more than the child of heredity and environment.

Keep your heart and life committed to God, no matter what or how much the suffering. Even in suffering, the Lord looks at you and says, "I see in you potential for greater happiness, friendship, and usefulness. These beautiful qualities can bloom in your life, and I will unfold them if you keep your life *yes* to me. I will make you a more wonderful person."

At one time, Jake was a senior partner in a prominent law firm. He began to drink heavily, and in the tailspin, he lost his family, position, everything. In that condition, Jake honestly gave himself and his life over to Jesus Christ and joined Alcoholics Anonymous.

Reluctantly, Jake was given a job with another law firm, not as a partner or associate, but at the low end of the totem pole. He was assigned the cases no one else wanted. One of them involved two companies who had spent hundreds of thousands of dollars and years of valuable time without re-solving their controversy.

Representing one of the companies, Jake asked counsel and representatives of the other company to meet with him. When they gathered, he startled them by sharing the dynamic change that had transpired in his life. Jake said, "If God can do that for a person like me, I'm sure he can help us resolve the problems before our corporations."

He shocked them again by suggesting that each one quietly pray for a few minutes, asking God for wisdom to settle the argument. They did as he suggested, and in thirty minutes, they arrived at a satisfactory solution.

Suffering need not suppress you! Rather, let it lead you to God, and let God lead you through it. Even if you floundered in the past, you can start anew *this* moment as an overcomer. You see, *this* moment is infinitely more important than the last.

When applying for renewal of her driver's license, one of my parishioners began telling the inspector how many years she had driven and without a single accident. The inspector interrupted, "Pardon me, lady, I'm really not interested in how you drove in the past. What I'm trying to find out is how you drive *today*." It's that way in life. By focusing on the present, you'll have more power than you've ever dreamed.

4. Beat Boredom

*You will gain unusual power if you add meaning
to your vocation.*

Judson Gooding, an American writer, stated, "Despite its
extraordinary variety of diversions and resources, its frenzy
for spectacles and its feverish pursuit of entertainment,
America is bored." [1] He claimed that our efforts to counter
boredom have defeated ourselves and boredom has become
the disease of our time. It can paralyse our actions and de-
press our minds.

A teenager takes dope because he's bored. Adults depend
on alcohol in an attempt to get rid of a bored feeling. Husband
or wife gets involved in an affair because of boredom with
the marriage partner. In their leisure years, senior citizens
develop a horde of ailments because boredom stalks their
lives.

People have found that boredom and emotional and physical tension are brothers. Boredom produces a greater feeling
of fatigue than hard manual labor.

As I waited to board a plane in Texas, several airport employees sat down next to me. One said, "Man, I'm tired as a
dog, but I haven't worked that hard." In a few moments, he
added, "I'm bored. Maybe that's why I've been so worn out
lately."

The next time you feel all worn out, take inventory of the
cause—work or boredom? Boredom drastically affects your
reasoning powers. It interrupts, impairs, and even reduces the
ability to make intelligent decisions. Mistakes are more apt to
occur. Reflexes are slowed down. Delayed responses charac-
terize the bored person.

In addition, boredom causes a way of life that is unflavored.
Charles Eliot, president of Harvard a number of years ago,

said that after he became head of the university his job no longer offered interest or challenge. Nine-tenths of it, Dr. Eliot claimed, became routine and dull.[2]

Boredom is a blight in the lives of many people even though more of us work today than ever before. We make more money now than at any time in the past, and in spite of taxes and inflation, more money remains for more things than we have ever known. But what about enjoying our prosperity? Joy is broken by boredom. From where does this boredom come?

Boredom is a state of mind. It is self-generated usually by a lack of meaningful, creative activity and a low sense of self-worth. In other words, people are bored from within. Did not Jesus say that out of the heart flow the issues of life?

However, your state of mind can be changed. In turn, your attitude on and off the job will change. What is the secret?

Ten Powerful Boredom-Breakers

Recognize the truth that you can change. "If I had a different job, a better job, then I would make more money and become a better person." Maybe. You have the responsibility to better yourself and your lot when opportunity presents itself, but it is not necessarily true that you need a different job. "Things" aren't primarily the cause of "things."

When our children were young, people advised my wife and me to get a bigger car. We had a little two-door Ford coupé that was four years old. Besides, they suggested, I needed a car with lots of leg space to accommodate my six-foot-six frame. They also said we needed a new car with some luxury and class. They were right. Furthermore, Mrs. Ray knew that the cramped quarters in the backseat of our small Ford made the kids—shall we say—uncomfortable and incompatible! So we made the big leap and bought a Pinto . . . station wagon. The kids could keep the backseat up and each have a nicely contoured bucketseat to himself—separated, naturally, from the other. Or they could put the backseat down and have more than enough room to stretch out on a nice, carpeted floor. Guess what? They managed to fuss anyway!

After about fifty miles of wall-to-wall ruckus one day, Mrs. Ray suggested I see what I could do. But before I did, she reminded the kids that even with a station wagon they weren't getting along.

A mumbler and grumbler will always find something to mumble and grumble about. Things don't complainers make. One's spirit does. The Lord said that out of the heart of man comes evil (see Matt. 15:18–19). The best answer to "if I had a different job" is a different person—a different you. A different person will make a job different.

As much as possible, make your job the job most suited to your abilities and desires. When a doctor who worked with lepers was asked if it was safe to work among the diseased, he answered, "If it's the place for you, it's the safest work in the world."

Jesus spoke about "the work which thou gavest me to do" (John 17:5, RSV). Your abilities and desires best suit you for a particular work and can be best used in that work. Inherently you are better suited for some work above all other work.

Over the fireplace in the Beverly Hills home of Fred Astaire is an old MGM interoffice memorandum that is a souvenir of the famous dancer's first screen test. It dates back to 1933, and it was sent by the testing director to his superior. The memo reads: "Fred Astaire. Can't act. Slightly bald. Can dance a little." Mr. Astaire proved the testing director wrong. However, his success depended a great deal on his doing, as much as possible, the work most suited to his abilities and desires. As a result, he had staying power.

See to it that your job is of value to others. For example, are you a truck driver or are you serving people by delivering cargo which requires talent and a truck? It does make a difference. "I glorify," Jesus said (John 17:4). He sanctified even the common tasks of life and transformed them into ways to benefit others. Theodore Roosevelt once said that no person needs sympathy because he has to work. One of the best prizes life offers is the chance to work hard at work worth doing. Worth depends on the value of work to others.

There is an old fable of unknown origin about a man who dreamed that he died and went to hell. He was surprised that he did *not* see fire and brimstone, which he expected. Instead, he discovered a great banquet table with food piled as high as the eye could see. Around the table sat the most miserable looking, emaciated people he had ever seen. As the man stepped closer, he saw the reason. Ten-foot-long forks were strapped to the arms of each person!

Later he dreamed that he died and went to heaven. There, too, was a great banquet table with food piled as high as the eye could see. But the men and women around that table looked happy and well-fed, although they too had ten-foot-long forks strapped to each arm. They were feeding each other!

A year-long study entitled, "Work in America," found that a significant number of American workers are unhappy with their work. The prescription offered is to "get a job that you enjoy and continue working at it as long as you possibly can." Investigators state, "The greatest single predictor of longevity is not how often one sees a doctor, but the extent to which one is satisfied with his work. Dissatisfying work is linked to heart disease and other physical and mental health problems." In conclusion, the report read, "Instead of a respected work role, we provide our older citizens with a sick role that encourages psychosomatic illnesses and excessive use of the medical care system." [3]

Is it not possible that American workers who are unhappy

with their jobs suffer from a sense that there is little or no real value for others in what they are doing?

If you have a sense of value in your work, you can go through misunderstanding and criticism and still keep your head high. "But," you apologize, "if I take that attitude, I might make a mistake."

You're right, but keep in mind that the Lord never called you not to make a mistake. He calls you to service. Benjamin Franklin went so far as to say that the person who does things makes many mistakes, but he never makes the biggest mistake of all—doing nothing. "Be doers of the word," wrote James (1:22, RSV).

People of action who want to be of value to others, as Wilfred Peterson, human relations consultant, stated, discover that life is a mixture of good days and bad, victory and defeat, give and take.[4] "Doers of the word" learn that it doesn't pay to let things and people get their goat, that they must let some things go over their heads like water off a duck's back. They learn that carrying a chip on the shoulder is the quickest way to get into a fight. They find that buck passing serves as a boomerang. They discover that carrying tales and gossip about others is the surest way to defeat. They find that giving others a lift by showing appreciation and praise is the best way to lift their own spirits. They learn that the world will not end when they make an error. They believe that there is another day and another chance. They discover that all men have burnt toast for breakfast now and then and that grumbling shouldn't get them down. They look for ways to benefit others, and the miracle is that by benefiting others they benefit themselves in some way, some time.

Increase your know-how. How important is knowledge of the job?

When George Washington was a young surveyor, he turned in a bill amounting to three hundred dollars for some work he'd done. The bill was returned unpaid; with it was a request that charges be itemized. Washington submitted the following: "Nails and stakes, $5.00; knowing where to put nails and stakes, $295.00."

Jesus was sure of himself: "[I have] accomplished the work" (John 17:4, RSV). Accomplishment demands know-how and increasing know-how. It's a process of continuing education at personal sacrifice and hard knocks.

A little boy in our area had long wanted a pair of ice skates. Although he had never been on ice skates before, he thought he'd like it, and he wanted his own pair on which to learn. He worked hard. Soon he had enough money to buy a set. With the skates tucked tightly under his arm, he made his way straight to the ice rink. He slipped them on and stepped out onto the ice. Ka-plop! He couldn't stay on his feet. He weaved, bobbled, and continuously in spread-eagle fashion with back-side down generously wiped the floor of the establishment!

Finally, a woman who had been observing the spectacle for a considerable time asked why he didn't take the skates off and go on home. "Because," he protested, "I didn't get these skates to give up with. I got them to learn how with."

Life is one big schoolhouse. Learn! Learn more! And more! That keeps you growing and makes you an asset. "The way to win," said Robert Lund, a top executive in one of America's largest corporations, "is to get out in front and improve your position. When you're green you're growing, but when you're ripe you're next to rotten." It is never too late to increase your know-how or, as Mr. Lund stated it, "improve your position."

Give EE: Extra Effort. Henry Irving became a great Shakespearean actor. When he first began in the theater, according to a critic, Irving had everything against him. He couldn't speak, walk, or sing. He wanted to do parts, but he could not. His amazing power was imprisoned. Only after years of dedicated work did he succeed in setting it free. Extra effort made the difference, but often we're like a recruit who tries to give less effort.

When I was in the navy, the company chief walked in the barracks and bellowed to seventy-eight of us recruits, "Anybody know shorthand?" Two burr-headed volunteers stepped forward thinking they'd get out of the grueling drills and hot sun that day. "Well," said the chief, "go help peel potatoes in the mess hall. They're shorthanded today."

EE is a rewarder. John Duff began working in a supermarket as a box boy. When something requiring EE needed to be done, the manager could count on John who gave EE without growling or complaining. As a matter of fact, I observed him, and I can verify that he did it freely and joyfully. He looked at a job that demanded extra effort as an opportunity, and he grabbed at it.

In a relatively short period of time, John was promoted to egg boy. His responsibility was to receive and carton the thousands of eggs sold each week by the store. Then he became a stocker, and later, a checker. Today he is regional manager and a vice-president of the chain. The president said, "One thing we can always depend on as far as John is concerned. He gives extra effort with an enthusiasm that encourages everyone around him."

EE is necessary because every worthwhile job takes oomph-plus. There are times when you have to give a little bit more.

Give ET: Extra Time. Let the clock free you rather than restrict you. It is there to set you loose instead of imprison you. Some people go to work to get off work. They are prisoners of the clock; yet even when they are off—"freed by the clock"—they don't feel like they're off. Jesus never punched a timeclock. Neither did George and Virginia Bush.

George was responsible for maintenance at a church I pastored. He was one of the most capable, all-around men on his job I have ever met. We used to say, "There's nothing

George can't do." His wife, Virginia, worked in the day school. So loved was she by the preschool children that they were anxious to be with her. *"Our* Mrs. Bush," they'd say. One of the Bushes' most amazing qualities was that when a job needed to be done the clock didn't keep them from doing it. They were willing to give the time necessary to finish the task, whatever it required. Therefore, they made time work for them.

This is a key to freedom from boredom. Make time work for you by giving ET.

Talk up your job. There is something magic to such talk. Up-talk improves mental climate and environment, and it stimulates others.

You throw a rock into a pond. You watch the stone drop into the water. You see the ripple begin. You look as it spreads out in all directions. So it is with up-talk. So it is with down-talk, except the effects are negative. It defeats and ultimately destroys unless it is stopped. When you down-talk your work, or anything, and keep talking it down, you separate yourself from it emotionally, mentally, and spiritually. Your work is no longer yours. You've alienated yourself. Consequently, you belong to it as a slave to a master.

You say there are conditions about your work that you don't like. If they are predominant and negative, you will have to find another place of employment or a new vocation. More than likely, those conditions aren't a majority. The question is, Can you still talk up your job? Of course, because you can talk up what excites you about your work. One of the biggest keys to positive employment is to praise the part of your job that draws praise out of you. Possibly these ideas will help.

1. Include words of praise when things are going against you. In her autobiography, Dale Evans discusses the tragic loss of Robin, Debbie, and Sandy, three of her children. Robin was a mongoloid child. Debbie died in a bus accident. Sandy died while in the service.

Such realities are never easy to face; yet Dale said that she knew better than to let bitterness get the best of her. In her own words, "The illnesses, the tragedies of my life and the disillusionments have served as spiritual correction of my soul." Furthermore, "the tears [God] has allowed . . . have cleared the eyes of my soul." [5]

That's the higher side of adversity.

As you include words of praise when things go against you, those words draw a picture of thankfulness. They are verbal descriptions that incline you toward better conditions. Therefore, they are situation-improvers and circumstance-changers. In either case, adversity becomes an advance.

2. Substitute praise for hostile and irritated feelings. Sometime ago when I was in Wichita, Kansas, to speak, one of those Plains' northers blew in. It was the first of the season and was it cold!

In the afternoon, I walked briskly the two blocks from the hotel to a store downtown. It was so cold that another half-block and I believe I would have been frozen. That evening we were at the beautiful, new civic center, and it was cold. One-third of the expected crowd was there.

A projector we were using blew out.

The mike I had around my neck broke as I was speaking. I had to grab and catch it before it slammed to the hardwood floor of the stage.

I began to feel belligerent and aggravated. Just then this thought came to mind: "Praise God anyway. Go ahead and thank the Lord." Praise as a substitute is a genuine substitute. It is infinitely superior to hostility and irritation. They hamper; it helps!

3. Visibilize your praise. Historians tell us that our Pilgrim ancestors put five grains of corn on each empty plate before they ate the Thanksgiving meal. They explained to their children that their forefathers had come to such desperate straits that there was an allowance of five grains of corn to eat each

day, but they were grateful and showed it. The grains visibilized their thankfulness.

What does visibilized praise do? It opens up your faith. It enlarges your eyes to gratitude so that you will see more for which to be thankful. It draws elements to you for which you can offer more praise.

4. Praise God instead of criticizing people. The reason is really quite simple. God always deserves praise, and people can always be criticized. A person inclined to be critical has no difficulty finding something about someone to criticize. When you begin to criticize, when you feel that old spirit coming on, catch yourself and say, "Praise you, Lord, for (name some good you see or that comes to mind that moment)."

5. Stick to praise. Any way you look at it, *endurance* is the magic word of success. Who's the winner?

The one who goes one down longer.

One round more.

One day.

One hour.

One minute.

One second.

One yard.

One foot.

One inch.

I know a man who gave fourteen of his best years to a business that was swept under in a recession. Friends treated him as if it were his funeral. He was taken aback, of course, and stung, but he knew there was power in enduring. After a brief rest-and-planning vacation, he began to build again. At the age when many people fold under the force of such adversity, Aaron began a new career—"God's way of beginning me over," he'd say! By staying with an attitude of praise, he forged ahead.

Praise, like life, calls for staying power; therefore, never give up praise.

Work as if you were working for God. Have to change your job? No longer can you be an attorney, teacher, clerk, waitress, housewife, salesman, engineer, truck driver, gardener, or executive? To work for God, you may think, is to become a professional minister, but that is far from the truth.

I spent several hours in the home of a postman who has been a rural mail carrier for over thirty years. Proudly he showed me his garden with its rows of corn, beans, onions, radishes, and cantaloupe. But even more important to him was his life. "I'm honoring God by what I'm doing," Mr. Baker said.

Carrying the mail has become a means by which he ministers. "I know Mrs. Jones is having a problem with her son," he said, "so when I pull up to put mail in her box, I'm reminded to pray for them.

"And Mr. Williams has been down with arthritis for months. Linda, the Whites' daughter, is having marriage problems. When I leave the mail in their boxes, I leave a prayer too for God's blessings on them."

This man works for God, not just the government.

God's ministers are God's people on God's earth doing God's will with their lives. God's ministers are not that nice, small clique called the clergy. It includes them, but in addition, you, dedicated to Jesus Christ, are a minister! You dedicated to Christ are the church in the world.

For whom are you working? "I have a family," thinks one person. "And I two children in college," says another. "I have to keep bread on the table." "Wife and I are working for the senior years we've always wanted." Then there's the ever-present "I have bills to pay."

At the deepest level you know, is God your working partner? "I bring you, Lord, honor on earth. I am accomplishing the work you give me," Jesus said (see John 17:4). If so, you are working for God.

Put some variety in your life. In his book *The Magic of Thinking Big,* Dr. David Schwartz says that executives today realize that what happens on weekends and between 6 P.M. and 9 A.M. directly affects a person's performance between 9 A.M. and 6 P.M. People who have a constructive off-the-job life are more effective than people who live in a bored family situation.[6]

It is advisable to plan your off-hours. Do constructive things. Vary the routine as much as possible.

Get the other nine boredom-breakers into action today. If these boredom-breakers are good for you, they need to begin now. Waiting for tomorrow before you use them is an escape from reality and a cause of workaday anxiety. It is procrastination. An unknown poet put it this way:

He was going to be all mortal should be—tomorrow.
No one should be kinder nor braver than he—tomorrow.
A friend who was troubled and weary he knew,
Who'd be glad of a light and who needed it, too.
On him he would call and see what he could do—tomorrow.

Each morning he stacked up the letters he'd write—tomorrow.
And thought of the folks he'd fill with delight—tomorrow.
It was too bad, indeed, he was busy today,
And hadn't a minute to stop on the way;
More time he'd have to give others, he'd say—tomorrow.

The greatest of workers this man would have been—tomorrow.
The world would have known him had he ever seen tomorrow.
But the fact is, he died and he faded from view,
And all that he left here when living was through
Was a mountain of things he intended to do—tomorrow.

Today's action needs to be taken today, and you'll begin to beat boredom on and off the job. You'll experience the joy of a powered person.

5. Discovering the Real You

You will achieve more power than you ever dreamed if you unearth the honest-to-goodness you.

Some housewreckers in Alexandria, Louisiana, found out too late they were demolishing the wrong house. Half the roof was removed, all the front porch was gone, and the upstairs of the two-story house was leveled. Then the owner happened to drive by. As he scurried up to the workers, he screamed, "What in heaven's name are you doing?" The foreman called his office and found out they should have been two blocks farther down the street.

When you think about it, that event is not as unreal as it sounds. People live in such unreality every day because they haven't discovered a strategy of life that satisfies. Consequently, they are not experiencing genuineness. They have yet to become real persons.

Unrealness results from alienation. Dr. Reuel Howe, the noted author, wrote that man's deepest need is to be at one with someone. The need grows out of a sense of alienation that exists within and between people, as well as between people and God.[1]

I am rather shocked and dismayed over the suicides among the college youth of our nation—young men and women with much life to live. Among the collegiate ranks, only death by automobile accident outnumbers self-inflicted death, and the percentage is growing faster than the population. What is at the bottom of this dilemma? An unreal self. It is the trauma that results when people haven't uncovered a real you, when they haven't begun to enjoy their amazing selves.

"Wait a minute," you insist. "I'm living in a crazy, mixed-up world. It's unreal! So what can I expect?" You can expect to

start becoming a more real person where you are. One of the
deepest thrills in life is to become a real person even when
things seem unreal. Then in a new and wonderful way, you
commence to overcome. Here's a thirteen-step program by
which to become a real person.

Be honest with yourself. Leading authorities in the study of
human characteristics agree that dishonesty in any form robs
a person of the ability to enjoy life. It siphons off self-esteem.
Persons who are unhappy with themselves are unhappy with
the world around them. Polly Bergen, an entertainment personality, said that she is mainly trying to be honest with those
around her and that the thing people find most difficult is
being honest with themselves.

Some people have the notion that honesty hurts, that it will
damage them, and that dishonesty heals. Nonsense! Honesty
heals; dishonesty hurts.

Other people fear the truth. When you fear something, you
automatically try to avoid it or hide from it.

I am not suggesting that it will always be painless to be
honest with yourself and to face the truth. As a matter of fact,
it may be painful. I asked a six-year-old girl what she thought
of our church service. She answered, "The music was OK,
but the commercial was too long."

On Sunday morning, the ministers wear robes. One Sunday
I walked into a kindergarten class with my robe on. Afterward
a mother relayed to me her son's report. "Mommy," he said
excitedly, "something visited us today. It wasn't a witch, and
it wasn't a clown. I don't know what it was." Honesty may be
painful, but you can depend on these facts: Honesty is good
for you! Honesty is rewarding! You're always ahead when
you're honest!

Restore wrongs. Realness requires you to acknowledge that
others are persons, that they have feelings, and that you must

act responsibly toward them. However, restoration for a wrongdoing does as much for you as for the other person. Unresolved wrongs blemish your personality. A guilt hangover nags you constantly.

"Dear Reverend Ray," began the letter, "Enclosed is a check for $100. Will you cash it and send to the minister at First Congregational Church. When I attended there, we didn't have a spare penny. A few times, I took money from the offering plate. It was never much and as far as I know, the money was never missed. Our family moved to another city five years ago. Since then, I prayed for forgiveness, but now I know I must also make restitution. The $100 is probably twice as much as I took."

How marvelous! The restorative process works miracles between people and in the person doing it. The outward act symbolizes inner activity—cleansing.

A man's neighbor asked if he had finished using the shovel.

"What shovel?" he questioned.

"Well, I loaned your son my shovel, and I need it to do some work."

The man replied that he didn't have the shovel and that he hadn't seen it. With that, both men forgot about it. About two months later, the shovel was found in a clump of bushes in the man's backyard. He didn't return it at the time although he knew it must belong next-door. It was a case of procrastination and negligence. Weeks later, he returned the shovel. "What a feeling," he told me. "It was like a laundry job in my heart."

Rise to your possibilities. To become a real person, you must believe you are blessed with genuine possibilities. You have potential you've probably not dreamed of, much less used. Possibilities unimagined, unexplored, unutilized!

A lady I know hates to get up in the morning. When I asked her why, she said, "There isn't much to get up to except boredom."

I replied that it doesn't need to be that way. When she looked puzzled, I explained, "You're young. There are many years ahead of you. Maybe you ought to think about going to college."

"Oh," she answered, obviously surprised, "I don't have enough brains to do that." I assured her that basic potential, application, and persistence are more important than IQ.

A man who is president of three corporations ranked 578 out of 580 graduating seniors. Fred went into service and did so-so there. Upon his discharge, he enrolled in college! Fortunately, there was one which would accept him. The first semester he struggled through with a C average. The second semester, he had a B or two. In his sophomore year, he managed three or four B's. He maintained a B average throughout his junior year and all A's in his senior year.

Fred has an average IQ, but he is rising to the possibilities his Lord has given him. He applies and persists!

Do the same and you'll be surprised at what you, together with God, will become and accomplish. Start achieving! You can probably think of a thousand excuses, but cast them aside. They are just what they're called—"excuses"—and excusers wallow in a mire of defeat.

Set your heart on a goal. Begin thinking, believing, and working toward it. Egotistical and selfish? No. It should take your thoughts to God and increase your faith, for your possibilities come from the Lord. It should lead you to appreciate him and yourself more than ever. It should increase your devotion to the Master.

Redeem the time. Use time as a gift. That's exactly what it is. What you do with it represents you as a person—who you are, what you are, and the value you place on yourself, others, and life. You think that opportunities for you are dulled? maybe nonexistent? not as good as they used to be? That's erroneous thinking. You were born in the middle of history.

If you are forty years old today, more has developed in your lifetime than in all recorded history prior to your birth. According to leading thinkers, more will be developed in the next twenty years than in all of recorded history prior to now. Opportunities unlimited are yours! When you use the time God has given you to take advantage of opportunities presently before you, you become a more real person by expressing God through the positive use of time.

Make changes in your personality. You can change! You need not be a victim to earlier conditioning, unpleasant experiences, and a negative environment. You can overcome handicaps. It is not necessary to be a sacrifice on the altar of heredity, powerless to redirect your destiny. You have a divine inner capacity which enables you to be more than you are.

Were you to stand before God today, you would not be asked why you weren't Moses, Jesus, St. Paul, Socrates, Shakespeare, Abraham Lincoln, John Kennedy, Lyndon Johnson, Pope Paul, Billy Graham, Henry Mancini, John Wayne, or Ralph Waldo Emerson, rather, why you weren't "you"? That is the person God will lead you to become.

Some try to do it by themselves, and they fail. They have the same old in-the-rut, frustrated, dead-ended, uneventful, uninteresting, ho-hum lives. They wonder why things don't work out. The reason: They substitute lonely self-effort for God-effort. They work *for* rather than *because of, in order to get* rather than *as a result.*

The James-Lange theory will be helpful to effect a change for the better: If you check or change the expression of your emotion you thereby change the emotion itself. The power is in your hands to change your personality; there is power available to do it.

Do what you know to do. As a third-grader, I had the responsibility of standing at the entrance to the cafeteria of

Travis Elementary School in Abilene, Texas, to make sure every kid put a quarter or ticket for lunch into the basket I held tightly with both hands. That was near the end of World War II, and bubble gum was scarce. That day, however, the little store across from school received an unexpected order of Double-Bubble. The news spread like a prairie fire throughout Travis School, but guess what? I didn't have any money with me, not even a penny. However, I did hold the straw basket into which a few quarters were being tossed.

On the screen of my mind, I saw the Double-Bubble. I saw myself blowing a gigantic bubble. Mentally, I heard it pop and saw it splatter all over my freckled face. Out of the corner of one eye, I took note of a quarter just dropped into the basket and thought, "No one will ever miss it." Oh, yes, I knew what to do—leave it where it was. What do you think I did? Through the terrifying agony of temptation, I left the quarter there!

Many people worry about the unknown; so they're troubled. But Jesus said, "You know these things—now do them! That is the path of blessing" (John 13:17, LB).

What do you know? You know to get rid of unbelief, cheating, cursing, swearing, thanklessness, dirty habits, filthy speech, negative thoughts, lying, lust, greed, indifference to responsibility, closed eyes to opportunities, disregard for self-discipline, resentment, bitterness, unforgiving spirit, jealousy, deceit, selfishness, hypocrisy, and mediocrity. "But," you think, "I cannot."

Yes, you can! It isn't a case of capability or copeability but willability. Are you willing? "We are more than conquerors through him who loves us." "We can do all things through Christ who strengthens us."

Look at difficulties as opportunities. A difficulty is an opportunity disguised in problematical clothing; it is common to see only the dilemma. Mary, a woman in the Midwest, saw the possibilities in every problem. In her late thirties, she lost her only child and the last living member of her family. He was killed in Vietnam. It's hard to see how good can come out of a situation like that, but she said that it had. She was able to help a couple who lost their only child in Vietnam.

They became bitter, resentful, sulky, depressed loners. They hardened to all attempts by friends to encourage them. The couple blamed God for the loss. In their minds, he was the savage god. Before their son's death, they loved to sing, but after his death, they could hardly stand hearing songs of joy and hope.

A special service was held in Mary's church to honor area residents who served in Vietnam. Her minister asked if she would share how her faith helped her through the loss of her boy. Mary not only accepted but invited her friends to attend. She was thrilled when she saw them in the crowd at the service.

As she spoke, Mary mentioned the unusual feeling that swept over her when she saw the officer who came to her door to tell of her son's death. The husband, sitting nearly at the back of the auditorium, let out a shriek loud enough that others in the sanctuary could hear. Tears flowed down his wife's grief-stricken face. At the close of the service, the minister invited people to come forward and kneel at an altar of prayer. That couple came and let God change them.

Instantly, there was a marked improvement in personality, attitude, and action. Immediately, they were outgoing and friendly. "He started smiling again," Mary emphasized, "greeting people, and he became active in the church again." The dynamics of a renewed person were evident.

The difficulty designed to defeat you hasn't been invented yet! Look for the possibilities in your problem. Perhaps you'll uncover more possibilities if you talk over the problem with a trusted friend, minister, or counselor. This will help keep the problem under your control; otherwise you will come under its control. This will help you maintain a more objective view.

Table transference permanently. In other words, stop pass-ing the buck. People try to transfer to others what pertains to them—a crafty, human trick used from time immemorial. The transfer may be total. Reaction to a sermon is a classic exam-ple. "That really hit old so and so, didn't it?" "Brother, didn't he speak to ____ today." Or it may be partial transference in which case you make sure you include others in the need.

A couple in their late twenties came to see me. For about thirty minutes they discussed their problems. Each concluded by saying that their marriage was hopeless, and each blamed the other. "She's cold, temperamental, and uncontrollable," he stated. "She's responsible for our fouled-up marriage."

"He won't talk to me; he's unconcerned and doesn't under-stand," she insisted. "I can't live with a person like that."

Such a response comes from a fear to face the music your-self. As a result, you seek out company to face it with you. However, as far as your own good is concerned, you have to face it yourself, as tough as it may be.

Ice isolationism. Personal isolationism is a by-myself rou-tine that works against your best interests. Dr. O. Hobart Mowrer, in his book *The New Group Therapy,* claims that "a man is never whole until he is 'open to the world.' This is not to say that a person has to shout his sins 'from the house-top.' Not at all. But he is not fully . . . out of danger until he is *no longer afraid* of having anyone know the truth about him."

Dr. Mowrer claims that "guilt is the fear of being found out and punished. The original sin (first wrongdoing) is com-pounded by deception, which becomes an ongoing 'sin' which was not merely committed then, but is still being practiced and perpetuated, here and now." [2]

Along the same line, Dr. Sidney S. Jourard wrote: "Every maladjusted person is a person who has not made himself known to another human being, and in consequence *does not know himself.* Nor can he be himself. More than that, he struggles actively to avoid becoming known by another human being. He works at it ceaselessly, twenty-four hours a day; and it is work." [3]

Dr. James R. Dolby in *I, Too, Am Man* states that to tell another person of one's own failure, guilt, insecurities, lust, and love may be as difficult a task as a person will ever have in his entire lifetime.[4] It has been said that some people would rather die than be known. The Bible says, "Confess your sins to one another, and pray for one another, that you may be healed. The prayer of a righteous man has great power in its effects" (James 5:16, RSV). I do not claim to know the full meaning of that verse, but it certainly refers to putting aside isolationism.

When you are no longer afraid to be known, you unlock a new freedom to living, a new happiness. You move from the edge of life into the eye of it.

Admit you're wearing a mask. You justify the façade by reasoning: If people know me—the real me, the actual person I am inside—they won't like me. If they don't find me out, they will like me. So I will wear a mask; I will be someone other than me; I will fool them, and they will love me.

Deceit will lead where? Only to delusion! Deception ends up where? With defeat! Naturally, because it begins in defeat! Then what's the use of pretending? You have to live with yourself. Even if no one else recognizes the false front you try to maintain, you do, and that's enough reason to tear it down.

You cannot love a mask. You cannot communicate with a mask. You cannot inspire a mask. Take it off! Let God help you put on the real you.

Face up to your feelings. There's as little to be gained from pretending you don't have feelings as there is to wearing a mask. A man I know discovered this truth after he turned seventy.

We sat in his living room talking. He leaned over to me and whispered, "I want to tell you something I've never told a soul—not even my wife, and she's the reason I'm still alive. In the last few months, I've thought several times of taking my life."

The news surprised me. He was one of the leading citizens in the area, and he did not want for the comforts of life.

"Why?" I asked. "Do you feel useless?"

"Exactly," he replied.

I assured him that retirement isn't a license to go out of gear. It's an opportunity to shift gears. But what impressed me the most was: He faced up to his feelings.

Do you want a big problem? Just lie to yourself about the feelings you have. Try to bury them. Act as if they're not. Sooner or later, you'll have to reckon with the consequences. The positive step is to face up to them. Having faced them, you're ready to handle them.

Accept God's unconditional love. How long have you thought that God is on a "you scratch my back and I'll scratch yours" system? The truth is, he will scratch yours even if you don't scratch his in return. That is the nature of divine love.

How often have you thought: How could God possibly love me after what I've done? The truth is, he loves the unlovable, especially the unlovable. That is the extent of divine love. Alex Thomas, a vice-president of the American Machine and Foundry Company, whose story I read in *Faith/At/Work* magazine, is a case in point.

Alex thanked the Almighty for material blessings, was honest in business, and tried to make sure his children got a solid education, respected their elders, and worked hard. A serious operation that put him down for ten weeks gave Alex time to think about his life. He began reading the New Testament, from a distance, so to speak, "from an intellectual point of view, careful not to become emotionally involved," as he put it. At Christmas time that year, he and his wife had a deluxe family argument "which was, of course, my wife's fault," Alex readily confessed. Through it he was brought face-to-face with the stark reality of utter spiritual failure.

When Alex confided in his minister, the pastor stunned Alex when he suggested that he "sign up with Christ's army." "This is what he had me write in my Bible," Alex said. "On this first day of January, I gave up my old way of life. I surrendered my life to Jesus Christ as my Savior and Lord. I am his forever and by word and by life, I will seek to lead others to know him." What happened?

According to Alex, "There was no burning bush, no heavenly host, no lightning inspiration. Instead there was an awareness of inner emptiness . . . and I set out honestly to fill that vacuum. My first objective was to get to know Christ better—if possible to make friends with him." To start, Alex set aside a quiet time each day during which he read a chapter from the Bible or from an inspirational book. Then he had a time of prayer and meditation during which he asked God to help open his heart to the Lord's love and will so that the day would be met in God's spirit. The quiet time required thirty to sixty minutes; therefore, he had to get up earlier. That wasn't easy at first, but after six years, Alex said it has become so essential that he rarely starts the day without it.

He witnessed that only by a complete acceptance of God's love could he be free. "Having laid my deepest self open to a friend who loved me, and having experienced the forgiveness offered by Jesus Christ, I was no longer afraid to be myself. I no longer have to pretend to be something I am not. And if I renew my relationship with God daily, I experience his presence, which relieves me of the guilt of yesterday and the fear of tomorrow." Yes, he has both feet in the world. He's very much involved in the "corporate jungle." He must make many decisions and deal with people. "The difference," Alex says, "comes when I let God take over." [5]

Accepting God's unconditional love at the deepest level you know will profoundly affect you. The real you begins to blossom, and isn't that what you actually want?

Defy delay—now! Don't put off adjustments. No more, "I'll change tomorrow." "I'll get things straightened out later." "I'll start becoming a real person after awhile."

Begin today! "This day I will begin" (Josh. 3:7, RSV). That word *begin* is thrilling. Vern Law used to pitch for the Pittsburgh Pirates. He also spoke some common sense when he said, "You will never reach second base if you keep one foot on first base."

There's an old legend about the devil wanting to destroy the church. Anger, a trusted lieutenant, volunteered to Satan. "I can do it," Anger said. "I'll make them mad at one another."

Then Greed volunteered. "Leave it to me," said Greed, "to make them devour themselves emotionally."

Jealousy said, "Oh, but Satan, I will destroy them through suspicion and distrust."

"And I," spoke up Despair, "will ruin them through pessimism. I'll get them to believing that there's no hope, that everything and everybody is bad. I'll make them give up."

Up walked Procrastination. "Satan, if you want a thorough job done, leave it to me. I'll tell them that they have a great job to do. I'll tell them that they can do it, that their God will help them to be successful, that their future is golden, that nothing can stop them." Just as Satan was about to doubt Procrastination's loyalty, the disciple said, "And I'll tell them they can begin *tomorrow*."

Today is the day God has made for you. This is the day to begin. No more delays, excuses, if's, or but's. Today. Spell NOW backwards, and you have WON.

The sooner you take that step, the better you'll be, the happier you'll become. You're on the way; you're gaining the power.

6. The Security
You've Been Searching For

*You will grow a new and exciting power if you
develop that certain sense of security.*

A sense of inner security is one of your basic needs. You want
to feel assured; you want to feel that you fit in; you want to
have a feeling of well-being. But you allow six areas to stymie
the development of security.

The Past

Unchecked, mistakes may have your life in nervous stitches.
Unresolved, they terrify and hypnotize you. "I shouldn't have
made that move," says a businessman. "It cost me my shirt."
"I should have taken that job," cries another. "Look where
I'd be today if I had."
Every counselor has heard similar stories.
In one way or another, every one of us has faced yesterday,
and we have found it necessary to come to terms with it.
Possibly the settlement you made is unfavorable to you. How
can you tell? By determining whether or not your security is
enriched or enfeebled.
1. Are you living satisfactorily with yesterday?
2. Are you living above yesterday?
3. Are you living in spite of the past?
4. Are you living in the past?
After I spoke at a service club one day, a man slipped out
of the crowd and grabbed my hand. "I want to tell you about
something that happened five years ago," he said. "Can you
spare a few minutes?"
We stepped over to the side, and I listened as this community leader explained how high ideals had been instilled in
him since childhood. "Thank the Lord for my parents," he

said. "Occasionally I felt they weren't 'up with the times,' but what they taught me saved my life."

Five years back, he was pulled in on a business deal that was dishonest, and he knew it was wrong. In the process, he took advantage of another businessman who was struggling. "A thousand and one voices within pointed fingers of guilt at me," he said. "In the heat of battle, I collapsed. When the chips were really down, I folded, and all for a few dollars!"

The heavy burden reflected on his face as he remembered the night he went off alone to think things out. "For several days, Becky [his wife] asked me what was the matter. She could tell something bothered me. I never was one to hide my feelings. The bad choice I made pierced my conscience like a hot iron. As never before, I faced the ugly past.

"So I got on a bus and started riding—nowhere in particular. Just riding. Several hours went by. Finally, I said, 'OK, Lord, I've made a big mistake, and I'll correct it as much as I can. Something happened down here. [He motioned to his heart.] Tears trickled down my face, but they were tears of joy!"

That very night he phoned the man of whom he had taken advantage. "Walter, I know it's kind of late, but I want to talk to you. May I stop by?"

When he got there, he apologized for the harm he had done. (You know, that isn't the easiest thing to do. Some people think it is a sign of weakness, especially in business circles. Of course, that is a mistaken idea!) The next day, he sent Walter a check for the amount he had made from the transaction.

One of the good results is that he helped Walter get on his feet again. Something else: Walter started to church and became a Christian too.

Do you see what transpired in him? He checked and resolved his downfall through *confession* (owning up to a wrong), *restitution* (righting the results of the wrong as much as he could), and *new living* ("I've never gotten into a dilemma like that again").

A place of tears was turned into a point of transformation! From tip to tip of his being, he tingled with release! A tomb was transformed into a tonic! A bomb was defused!

It is a wonderful thing to face life in the spirit of the man who lost his eyesight. He rushed to the physician. The treatment by the doctor made it possible for him to see again, but with the return of his sight, he lost his memory. He wasted no time in getting back to the doctor. This time he was treated for a loss of memory. The man regained his memory but promptly lost his eyesight again.

"Well," said the physician, "we can't cure both together, so you'll have to choose between sight and memory. Which will it be?"

The man answered, "Eyesight. I'd rather see where I'm going than to know where I've been." That's the high-level way to look at the past because the next step is much more important than the last step!

Age

It doesn't take a genius to figure out that we will all get older unless we die sooner. On unfounded reasons, people tend to think aging is a catastrophic development. Changes required by maturity are looked upon as liabilities. From forty on, some feel life is a downhill slide. When you stop to think that a big segment of the American people are in the forty-plus crowd, you can begin to assess the effect such dilapidated thinking has on national life. Add to it the influence on the business, education, and church life of the country which the forty-plus crowd exerts, and the damage of such an attitude is staggering.

One area in which the forty-plus crowd may feel a pinch is employment. After finding that their age has become a barrier to employment, many people undergo a traumatic gap in security. The price is paid in loss of income, spiritual misery, marriage failures, and social problems. Yes, there are inadequacies and faults in our employment system. Age discrimination is the worst!

The crises in the life of a person going through this experience are enormous. Just when the family is raised, he finds himself out of a job. When he has made it through the higher expense years and is ready to do some things he has always wanted, such as go some places he has always wanted to go and put away a nest egg for years ahead, he's unemployed.

The dilemma is made quite clear in the case of Tom, a college classmate of mine. It has been twenty years since he loaded Coca-Cola trucks to earn his way through school; nineteen years since he became a Navy ensign in the service of his country; and fifteen years since he began his career as an engineer. At age forty-two, Tom loses his job as an executive with the firm due to a colossal slump in the building industry. Nobody in Watts, Harlem, or on the reservation wastes any tears on Tom and the loss of his sixty-thousand-dollar-a-year salary. But the high-flying executives across America feel a tremor down the spine of their business backs.

In a sluggish economy, overqualified, luxury-laden, high-salaried Tom finds few firms willing even to talk with him. The odds are he will get a job, probably not at his last level, but at least a job, if he sticks with the hunting—in the next year or two.

What security is there, he wonders?

However, the end has not come for the Toms or anyone else unless they fold their hands and timidly surrender.

Jay came by to see me. Life vibrated from him. "Don't ask my age," he said.

After listening for awhile, I said, "You told me not to ask, but curiosity is getting the best of me. What age are you?"

"Seventy-two," he replied hesitantly but firmly.

After a rewarding career as vice-president of the Case Farm Implement Manufacturing Company and head of material procurement for NATO, this man was classified as one of the "over-the-hill" gang—an age dropout. Being full of faith and better sense, he began giving himself in further service to forty-plus people who think they have had it. What an amazing contribution he has been! He came by my office at the very time I was working on this part about age and security.

Confident that I might pick up some valuable help, I asked him what advice he would give those who allow age to threaten their security. "In the first place," he said sharply, "security is within. Actually, there isn't any security outside you. Furthermore, anybody can feel secure if his trust is in the Lord, if he really believes he is in this world for a purpose, if he admits he has some talents which can benefit other people, and if he is growing as a person."

Mary Starr was in the forty-plus crowd when her husband passed away. Abruptly, she found herself with a sinking manufacturing company on her hands. Everything she owned was threatened, including wide real estate holdings. Not one to toss in the towel without a gallant fight, she, plus God (indeed! God through her) pitched in. When the smoke cleared, the problems were resolved, and the business was intact. "Miraculously," she insists, "God pulled me through. Even if I had lost everything, I would still have him."

Such people have little problem with an age-geared security-gap. Today, Mary personally directs her broad real estate interests even though she has been a happy member of the sixty-five-and-over crowd for a long while.

Have you thought of a new career? I am serious! Yes, even when you are over forty! Possibly age is an opportunity for redirection. You could very well be surprised with new frontiers awaiting you.

An honest security age analysis is no respecter of years. Ask yourself:

1. Upon whom or what does my security depend? (If it is age, you either are a problem or have a problem, or both!)
2. Do I emphasize ability or age?
3. Do I sell profitability or years?
4. Am I a contribution?
5. Am I the kind of friend I would like to have?
6. Am I fun to be around?
7. Am I serious at the right time?
8. Do I make allowances for mistakes?
9. Am I becoming the full person I may become?
10. Am I a humble, self-confident person?
11. Do I accept change gratefully and advocate change when it is an improvement?
12. Do I welcome the maturing process certain that life can be wonderful at any time?

Yes, you are aging! Face it! I am too! But there is a striking beauty about it.

Demands

The load is too heavy; life is too much. The burden is too big; you think you can't bear it. You agree with the psalmist when he moped, "Problems far too big for me to solve are piled higher than my head" (Ps. 40:12, LB).

You may feel like the young man in Hugh Walpole's novel who says:

> You know there can't be a God, Vanessa. In your heart you must know it. You are a wise woman. You read and think. Well, then ask yourself. How can there be a God and life be as it is? If there is one He ought to be ashamed of Himself, that's all I can say.[1]

At least, you feel about the demand the way the young, worn-out mother felt when she said to her crying toddler,

"Tammy! Tammy! Tammy! Please go to sleep. I need your nap." You wonder: Where will I ever find the time? How can I possibly be expected to do this? Who do they think I am? Who, other than a fool, feels I can make it through this?

Definitely, your life may have balance. Life is tailored precisely for you, and you are tailored for life. The demands made of you are right for you. The hurry, worry, busy routine begins when you assume more than is meant for you. Dullness and laziness start when you assume less than is meant for you. Something wonderful is at work to give you this balance.

When you trust God, everything comes to you through him. One of the most helpful thoughts I have is of God as the Master Regulator. Near our house, a large reservoir collects melted snow and rain. The reservoir supplies thousands of families with water for baths, dishwashing, gardens, lawns, and personal consumption. The men responsible for the reservoir must release the water to treatment stations in proper proportions—no more, no less—and at the right times.

When the heavenly Father regulates your life, he controls the demands. You can be assured of measured release. Fred Steinmark was brought to my attention in December 1969. He walked into the University of Texas dressing room after helping squeak out a 15–14 Longhorn win over the University of Arkansas. As is his custom, Coach Darrell Royal led the squad in prayer. Then President Nixon presented a plaque honoring the football team. Freddie and the squad were headed for the Cotton Bowl on New Year's Day. Again, Freddie felt the excruciating pain in his left leg. It had hurt before, but now it was getting unbearable. Examinations on Monday revealed a growth. "Let's get a good look with a biopsy," the doctor advised.

On Wednesday, the specialist told Freddie that if the biopsy showed cancer the leg would have to go. "Lord," young Steinmark pleaded, "don't let this happen to me. Don't let it be cancerous."

"I knew that wasn't a prayer at all," he confessed. Then he prayed, "Father, I don't want to lose my leg, but if that's the way it must be, help me to bear it"—even though it ends dreams for a pro career in either football or baseball.

Friday morning, Fred went in for the biopsy, not knowing whether he would have both legs when the day ended. Eight hours later, he began to recover from the anesthesia, minus a leg. "Self-pity," Steinmark admitted, "could be a far greater handicap than losing a leg. I prayed for God to help me. He sure sent some wonderful comforters . . . 12,000 of them . . . cards and letters. . . . I have learned about a wonderful God who gives you strength and courage to overcome any obstacle."

That wonderful God helped him to be at the game on New Year's Day and on his new leg, walking, at the athletic banquet on January 12, about a month after the amputation. Five thousand people jumped to their feet and roared in appreciation as Fred walked up by himself to accept his varsity letter. "Great guy," said Coach Royal as he threw his arms around him. "You made it." Fred is making it because he discovered the power of measured release.

Up to now, you thought the requirements were too much. Well, they aren't! The resources available are more than sufficient for the demands.

Depreciated Self

Everyone needs to have an adequate concept of himself—who he is, what he is, his potential, possibilities, and reserves. But many of us suffer from a depreciated self-image and feelings of inferiority.

The depreciated self shows itself through abuses. Believe it or not, drug usage is an abuse. Dr. H. H. Barnette, a Los Angeles physician, claims that the motivation driving people to drugs includes a desire to escape from reality, a search for self-identity, the search for religious experience, a sense of meaninglessness, a desire for thrills, rebellion against parents, curiosity, inadequate family relationships, peer group pressures, oppressive social conditions, and a low self-image.

Happy and successful people, in the deepest sense, have many characteristics in common—motivation, goals, right attitude, and a positive self-image. The sense of depreciated self is filling the offices of psychiatrists. What damage does the depreciated self bring?

1. It makes you feel God doesn't care about you.
2. It represses your potential.
3. It suppresses your possibilities.
4. It makes you sorry to see another day.
5. It drains you of energy and enthusiasm.
6. It instills in you a fear of success as well as a fear of failure.
7. Sometimes mistaken for humility, it hushes the will to live, diminishes the drive to contribute, and thwarts the thrill of life you may enjoy.

The depreciated self is a big threat to your security.

Difficulties

I have met folks who let hard challenges stifle their security. Problems kayo them. The security of others is stiffened by difficulties. Richard Crooks is an example of them.

In spite of a miserably poor childhood, Richard Crooks became one of the outstanding tenors this nation has produced. In his youth, the family didn't have money for music lessons, but someone recognized that his untrained voice had unusual possibilities. At age twelve, Richard sang in a music festival.

"You have the voice of an angel," exclaimed an expert in the audience. This spurred the young man to find a way to train his voice. As a teenager, Richard worked in an ice plant to earn enough money for lessons. He got up at 3:00 A.M.

each day and began lugging ice. The time came when he was engaged as soloist for a New York church, and before long, he was a star with the New York Philharmonic. The poverty-stricken kid, ice-toting teenager became the outstanding tenor.[2]

As more than a few believing people have discovered, Mr. Crooks's difficulties deepened his security. They didn't destroy it! Two of life's grandest experiences can come through problems. (1) *We may learn truly great lessons.* Sometimes difficulties get us in the place where we are ready to listen. Then we learn, really learn! (2) *We can feel the force of God's touch to more than match the difficulties.* It is the divine reinforcement for living. There is a unique thrill to that.

Detachment

Detachment must be one of the most painful emotional experiences which can come to you. The heart aches; the mind questions if anyone cares; life seems standoffish.

Recently, I talked with a man who heads up one of the largest religious education ministries in California. When asked what success his church is having with adults on Sunday morning, he answered that if it weren't for the hundreds attending groups for single adults the department would look rather sickly. I inquired further about the success of the singles' groups. Why these people especially? He replied, "They are lonely, and they feel out of it. They sense a detachment, therefore, a strong need for one another."

A psychoanalyst friend maintains that urbanized America is quickly getting out of touch. As people lose attachment, security seems to fly out the window. They feel like the stub after going through a turnstile at Disneyland.

These threats to inner security appear colossal. You have a past. You are getting older. You have demands on your life. At one time or another, you have thought little of yourself. You have difficulties, and you have felt detached.

Can any intelligent person living in such days as these expect to be secure? A good question. We live in a universe where it would take 250,000 years just to count the atoms in a pinhead. Unknowns stagger our best brains. Times may be tough. Realities are raw.

Still, you may have security if you get to the heart of it and find out what security really is, where it takes place, and when you tap into the source of it.

Many centuries ago, a man struck a sure chord when he said, "Be strong; be brave. Do not let bad things or challenges strike terror or panic into your heart. You have God to help you" (see 2 Chron. 32:7–8). Another famous man felt it when he witnessed, "Because the Lord is my Shepherd, I have everything I need" (Ps. 23:1, LB). From a prison, St. Paul victoriously claimed, "I know in whom I am believing, and I am sure he will keep me" (see 2 Tim. 1.12).

First, last, and always, security is an inside job. You must have it in your spirit, soul, and mind. If it isn't there, you haven't got it. Your life may be crammed with things, but you won't have security until you respond from the need of the heart.

Security is actually a matter of the power of God being released in you. That is the only security, for God is the only unshakeable source. When the Almighty comes, he comes to be in you for life, bringing the security he is. God offers an answer, for he is *the* answer; and the one thing he wants more than anything else is to share the answer with you!

What response is adequate? Commitment. Rather than a fanatical, irrational, irresponsible expression, commitment is an experience of union; as best as you know, let go and let God. "Lord, here I am. I turn myself over to you. From this moment on, I'm yours." The result is an enrichment and increase of life beyond your wildest dream!

This gets to the heart. Like anything worthwhile, it requires decision. To say no is a decision to decline. To decline to say is a decision to decline. To say yes is a decision to accept.

The upshot of the yes-decision is performance, practical living with Christ at your side and within you. No longer is he "out there" somewhere. He comes near you and next to you for the business of living.

A man phoned and wanted to see me immediately. When he walked into my office, he was about ready to scuttle life. "I'm confused," he cried, "so confused. How can the God you talk about be afoot in a world like this?"

Still a young man, he had been through one marriage. "Didn't work at all," he explained.

I listened to his story patiently, and then I began to get in a few words. "Tom, do you want me to prittle-prattle with so much talk, or get to the point of it all?"

"Get to the point, reverend," he answered in that "Oh, me! Here-it-comes, let's get-it-over-with" tone.

"You've searched for fuller meaning in many places, haven't you?" He admitted a rather comprehensive search—free sex, some drugs, philosophy (he is a very educated man), theosophy, and a shallow cult or two. "And you haven't found it. I don't believe you ever will until you go to the Lord because he gives in here (the spirit) what it takes out there (life)."

"What do you mean?"

"In the words of G. K. Chesterton, until the 'natural connects with the Supernatural, you are unnatural.' You need to connect vitally with God."

I explained that faith is the connecting link. A person begins with an honest, open talk with the Lord, releasing oneself to him. From there, you really live! You perform. "I want this," Tom confessed.

In the next few minutes, I witnessed again the miracle of transformation and new beginning. Another human being had found the security he had always wanted and the immense power for which he yearned.

7. Looking for Serenity?
Here It Is!

You will achieve immense power of the inner self if you get peace and calm at the center of yourself.

You really want a sense of serenity that reaches to the heart of life and produces positive results. Remember the last time you were jittery inside? The boss wanted an eleventh mile out of you at the twelfth hour. A job couldn't possibly wait. Perhaps it was a big exam at school or children screaming from every keyhole. Possibly, you were hemmed in on all sides by motorists rushing down the freeway at breakneck speeds or locked in by hundreds of cars in a classic but routine traffic tie-up.

In a hurried, energy-blinding whirl, you may have thought of a lazily flowing stream or some beautiful woods where birds chirp soothing melodies and carefree animals scamper about. Oh, how you have wished for that!

Well, you are a serenity-seeker. That's good, for whether on Wall Street or in the woodlands, you were created with a built-in yearning for serenity. It's a requirement for meeting the day with enthusiasm. Dr. Alexis Carrel, the great French scientist, said that those who keep the peace of their own inner selves in the midst of the tumult of the modern city are immune from nervous diseases. He also said that people who don't know how to fight worry die young. (Worry, you know, usually accompanies agitated living.)

A good definition of serenity is: "peace of your inner self." The result is an unruffled spirit; yet on occasions it is hard to remain unruffled.

I have witnessed the miracle of inner peace many times, but none was more obvious than in the life of Bill Vaughn.

Bill, a few years ahead of me in school, was a popular football player. We developed a friendship while working together part-time in a grocery store. A likeable fellow with a crew cut, Bill was the girls' idol, but he had a terrible temper and was moody. When things didn't go exactly his way, he was nearly unmanageable, pouty, and highly emotional. After he cooled off and calmed down, Bill always felt like a heel over his attitude and conduct. "I know better," he would say in reflection, "but I found myself uncontrollable, I guess."

Although he had been attending church, Christianity hadn't gripped Bill seriously. The power of Jesus Christ hadn't been released through faith in Bill's mind and life. "One day," Bill told me, "I came to the conclusion that if religion were valid at all it was worth living 100 percent." In the quietness of a football-conscious teenager's room, Bill made an agreement with God. "Lord," he prayed, "I don't know much about you, but I know enough to want to live according to your will. And, dear God, the only way I can live your will is to go all out with you. Here I am, Lord. I'm yours. I promise, if you'll help, to live as if you are physically by me."

Bill's attitude began to change substantially; a friend described the change in Bill's countenance as a mental facelift. His actions and reactions, in the face of identical circumstances as before, became different. He was manageable, in control, in charge of his mind and emotions. Bill had become possessed by an unruffable spirit, and what a gloriously different and refreshing person he became. Bill, like any one of us can because of God's help, became an overcomer. He overcame annoying habits and anger.

The strength of serenity, however, is shown in victory over disturbances. It's an "in spite of" triumph, a "through all" conquest. "Be filled with his [God's] mighty, glorious strength so that you can keep going no matter what happens—always full of the joy of the Lord" (Col. 1:11, LB). That is the bigger view of serenity.

Remember, serenity is on Main Street, not withdrawn from life. Serenity is not cloistered behind locked doors and high, forbidding walls. It is not shut away from realities—whatever they are. Rather, serenity helps you cope with realities.

Can anyone doubt that serenity has tremendous impact on personal life? It brings a calmness of mind when circumstances are hectic. I am thinking of Frank who was the first baseman for his Little League team. Tall, handsome, and rythmic, this young man was impressive. One afternoon he taught a grandstand full of spectators, as well as his teammates, the power of a calm mind.

Often, the only thing a Little Leaguer need do in order to get on base is to meet the ball with a little wood or manage to stand at the plate long enough for a walk. It was that sort of afternoon for Frank's Cardinals. His teammates were letting easy grounders slip through into the outfield. They were dropping routine fly balls. Finally, when one of them happened to scoop up a grounder with bases loaded, he was so surprised that he froze with the ball in his glove. A run scored, and the bases were still loaded. Frank felt it was time for some straightforward action. "OK, fellows," he urged. "Calm down. Let's play ball."

The batter popped up toward second base. Although it wasn't his ball, Frank ran over and waved his teammates away. As poised as a pro, he caught the fly. "Settle down, men," he encouraged them. "Keep cool."

The next batter whacked a hard grounder between first and second. Frank played the ball and with ease threw it home to force the runner.

With two away and bases loaded, the batter smashed a line drive about three feet above Frank's head. Reacting with split-second timing, he leaped and came down with the ball firmly fixed in the net of his glove. His teammates surrounded him with boisterous cheers. "Way to go, big Frank! Way to go!"

From that point on, it was a different ball club and game.

Calmness restored order and sense to that ball team; it does to anyone.

Cool thinking adds a fuller dimension to life, and it helps you get through trying times without losing control of yourself.

Serenity also brings an evenness of temper. Hotheads lose. A man explained how he and his wife handled anger. When some people at the office complimented him on his deep, rich suntan, he said it was a blessing of their marriage. "At the time we said our vows, my wife and I decided that when she got angry I would go outdoors until things cooled off."

That inflamed emotions can dynamite your life is shown by a fatal accident which happened in my hometown. The driver had a heated argument with his wife. He stormed out of the house and got into the car. Emotionally distraught, he lost control of the automobile and crashed into the concrete siding of a bridge. One of the investigating officers, a member of my church, said it is regrettable that there is no way to keep a person who has temporarily lost control of his emotions off the road.

Serenity is the answer, but it cannot be legislated. Serenity will hold emotions in check.

1. Serenity makes it possible for you to do best what you want to do. (Deep down inside, you want a good outcome to what you do.)
2. Serenity makes it possible for you to say best what you want to say. (People in a dither find it difficult to convey their ideas as clearly as they want to.)
3. Serenity makes you more effective. (People are impressed when your demeanor is steady.)
4. Serenity reduces strain on your nerves. (They are pulled together, not apart.)
5. Serenity helps you get across your point without fuming. (A boil-over can be harmful—spiritually, emotionally, and physically.)

6. Serenity deepens friendship. (Calm people are good friends to have.)
7. Serenity helps you make new friends easily and hold on to them. (Your personality becomes a plus. People want to be around you.)
8. Serenity keeps you on top of circumstances. (It is powerful.)

Helen Keller is a marvelous example of the power of serenity. One of the most radiant and useful personalities of her generation, Miss Keller was blind and deaf. Still, she did much for mankind. The University of Glasgow recognized her outstanding contribution to humanity when it gave her an honorary doctorate. As they presented the award, the national anthem was sung. With the aid of her companion, Miss Keller kept abreast of the events and responded to the gathering. After thanking them, she closed with these words: "Darkness and silence need not bar the progress of the immortal spirit." According to reports, the crowd leaped to its feet in a standing ovation which Miss Keller could neither see nor hear. Her serene spirit overtook every obstacle and swept the crowd upward!

Four Steps to Serene Living

Serenity is a matter of the spirit, and it can be acquired, for it is the result of an input. The following steps have helped many on the road to serene living.

Quietness. People are noisy; maybe we are the noisy generation—monstrous jets, earth-shattering sonic booms, crunching machines, jammed freeways, and spine-rattling horns. We somehow believe that noise represents depth. Actually, the deeper a person is, the quieter he or she may be within. The noisy person is usually closer to the surface.

We also think we have to be loud to be heard. As always, an honestly quiet spirit bears a phenomenal victory.

With an eye made quiet by the power of harmony and joy, we see into the life of things. As Franklyn Sherman puts it, we become quiet enough to think about eternal verities and to home ourselves in God. ". . . experience God's peace, which is far more wonderful than the human mind can understand. His peace will keep your thoughts and your hearts quiet" (Phil. 4:7, LB). When quietness seems to be getting away from you, remember:

1. Things could be worse.
2. They aren't as bad as you think.
3. They can be much better.
4. It is a situation, and every situation can be handled successfully.
5. You have sufficient resources available.
6. You can find them.
7. Take them and use them.

Listen. As a twelve-year-old, our son Jerry finished several months of youth instruction classes after which he could have chosen to confess his Christian faith and unite with the church. "What do you think, dad?" he asked.

I assured him that is a decision each one needs to make for himself. Religion and church membership must be treated differently than an older brother's clothes. They aren't hand-me-downs. Of course, I outlined again what it means to become a Christian and live with faith in your heart. "I know I believe in Christ," Jerry said, "but I'm not sure this is the right time for me to join the church. Maybe I ought to wait until I'm a little older."

Sizing up the situation, I inquired if he had asked God what he should do about this very important matter.

"Ha! What do you mean? Yeah, God's going to talk to me? I bet!" He could just see some sort of spooky stuff going on.

His younger sister chimed in, "Yeah, dad, God can't talk!" This, of course, is not the case. Mr. Rank illustrates the reasonableness of listening within.

The Arthur Rank organization controlled England's entertainment industry. Mr. Rank distinguished himself as an astute problem-solver and accurate decision-maker. How did he do it?

Often he called his key executives together to lay out a problem. First, they clearly defined it, and then they discussed it. Mr. Rank would remain quiet as his men talked. When they wound down, he would call everything to a hush and close his eyes in complete silence. After awhile he would say, "Lord, now what do you want us to do?" Then there was another breathtaking silence during which Mr. Rank would listen. Maybe one minute. Five minutes. Fifteen minutes.

When Mr. Rank got the answer, he would open his eyes and announce it. Experts say that the results have been rather amazing. It brings to mind Proverbs 3:5–6: ". . . trust the Lord completely; . . . In everything you do, put God first, and he will direct you and crown your efforts with success" (LB).

Here are twelve rules for listening effectively.

1. Pause. (If you hurry, you may miss the wonderful results.)
2. Lean back in your chair and get comfortable. (Or you may prefer to kneel.)
3. Relax. (Let your body get loose. Dangle your arms. Turn your head from side to side a time or two so as to release your neck muscles.)
4. Take a deep breath and release it slowly. (Push the air all the way out.)
5. Take another deep breath easily; then resume normal breathing.
6. Close your eyes softly.
7. Explain your need to God.
8. Invite the Lord to take care of it his way.
9. Ask him to let you know what his way is.
10. Let your mind be filled with God's wisdom. (Want it.)

11. Be very still.
12. You may feel a desire to read in the Bible, perhaps to turn to a particular passage; or you may open the Bible up to a verse that applies exactly to your need at that moment. (Keep a Bible handy. It is your source book.)

Do what you can about an upsetting situation. You are prepared to do this when your heart is quiet. The situation may be upsetting, but you will not be upset! That is essential to success. You are not meekly folding your hands in an "I'm not involved" manner, nor are you saying, "I don't care." Rather you are doing whatever you can, however small the effort might seem. Realizing that you are an individual with unique possibilities, you lend yourself to the answer, as did Gladys Aylward in China.

Miss Aylward was so small that when she sat in a chair her feet didn't touch the floor. Years ago, she stood and listened to a Salvation Army service conducted on a street corner in London. She was moved to become a Christian.

The family for whom Miss Aylward kept house had an excellent library on China. She began reading, and the more she read, the more fascinated she became with that ancient country. One day her employer saw her reading. "Who gave you permission to use my books?" he scolded her, but finally he said, "OK, you can read the books, but only after you've done all your work."

Miss Aylward felt the call of God to go to China as a missionary; so she applied to a missions board. Although she failed the board's test, she believed God called her to go and go she did. On the streets of Yangcheng, she told people that the power of Jesus Christ is the greatest power in the universe, that a Christian need not be overcome by anyone or anything. "Overcome through faith," she preached week after week.

One day the governor called her to his office. "We have a

horrible dilemma," he said. "In one of our prisons, there is a vicious riot where murderers are in control. One of them is berserk. Already he has killed two men with a meat cleaver. We want you to go in and take the cleaver from his hands."

"Me?" she questioned. "You must be crazy!"

"You've been telling us," replied the governor, "that your Christ is always with you—like Daniel in the lions' den. You've said that your Christ protects you."

"But," argued Miss Aylward, "you don't understand."

The governor answered, "Then you haven't been telling us the truth, huh. I listened to you and believed you."

She knew she had to do what she could about an upsetting situation; so she asked the Lord to guide her. After walking in the prison door, she found herself in a narrow tunnel. At the end of it, she saw the prisoners running around shouting and cursing. "Jesus," she prayed, "I believe you are with me. I claim victory."

She walked on. She saw the mad prisoner and the meat cleaver dripping with blood which he held in his hand as he chased another man. Suddenly, she was face-to-face with him. The wild and terrifying eyes of the prisoner were met by Gladys Aylward as she calmly instructed, "Give me that cleaver." After a moment of stunned silence, he meekly handed it to her. "All right," she said, "all of you men get in line—now!" They quietly obeyed. "Let me hear your complaints and I'll give them to the governor." [1]

Through the divine wisdom you get when you are quiet inside, you discover a course of action you may take. Whatever else may be done, certainly you can pray, and prayer is a mighty mountain-mover.

Trust the matter to the Lord. What greater act can you do while you are doing what you can? What more can you do after you have done what you can?

One time an embarrassing situation involved my name even though I was not responsible for the unfortunate development.

Without delay, I made numerous contacts, exhausted every effort, and applied strenuous pressure to clear it up. Yet the predicament went from bad to worse. I was utterly disgusted and humiliated and almost ready to blow up. Then I realized I had done what I could. Now I must trust the entire thing to God. That was a source of relief and, I might say, action. The matter was cleared up.

By trusting the situation to God, you get the problem into bigger hands. A remarkable woman, Frances Gardner, suggests a helpful way to do this.

1. Pray about it, and as you do, stretch your hand as far out in front of you as you can. Symbolically you are reaching out to God.
2. Turn the palm of your hand up keeping your fingers separate. You are offering the matter to the Lord. If it is a big thing, use both hands, cupping them together.
3. Flip your hand over, palm down. Now, you are releasing it into God's hand. You are prone to hold on to things yourself. Or you hang on to a bit of it. You pray, but you keep a finger in it. When your hand is turned over and your fingers separated from one another as far as possible, you cannot hold anything in your hand.
4. Keep your hand open. Do not clench your fist by which you would hold on to the matter.
5. Drop your hands to your side. Do not pull them back to your chest. If you do, it symbolizes you are taking it back after you have offered it to God and supposedly let it drop into His hand. Often that is what we do. We pray, we offer, and we bring it back to us. Instead, let your hands fall to your side.
6. Thank God for hearing and helping you.[2]

This method will work in your private life, in your business, family, marriage, relationships, sales—anything, anywhere!

The quest after a serene life leads people in many directions.

Not long ago, three hundred members of a Los Angeles church decided to seek the serene life elsewhere. They quit their jobs, sold their homes, left friends, completely uprooted their lives, and moved away. According to a man in the group, they were tired of "the hustle and bustle" of Los Angeles.

I know a man who decided that serene living and city life do not mix. "The pressures of business are too much," he told me. So he got rid of his appliance company and moved the family to a lovely hideaway up north. Eight months later, he returned to Los Angeles. "I guess I was wrong. It is beautiful up there, and it helps to spend a few days there once in awhile, but I discovered that what I'm looking for is not found in a place. It must be in the heart. If that is so, we can have it even in Los Angeles!" He is right! And if in Los Angeles, then every city, village, and hamlet in the world!

Psalm 37 paints a remarkable picture of this. Don't get bothered at other people, even those who are doing bad yet seem to be getting much farther ahead than you are. What may you do instead?

1. Trust in the Lord. (You are always in front when you do and behind when you don't.)
2. Be delighted with the Lord. (Have fun living the way he wants you to. Really, life need not be dull and defeating when God is with you. His way is always best—and more thrilling.)
3. Commit everything you do to the Lord. (Abundant purpose will fill each day.)
4. Rest in the Lord. (Let him help you, and constant energy will be yours. By yourself, you will fizzle and fall.)

If this seems overly religious, that is where genuine serenity is. The person who is tied to his own bootstraps has no reserves other than what he can singlehandedly put together. On occasion he will find himself seriously in need of deeper reinforcements to meet the challenges on his hands. In the absence of adequate reserves, he comes unseamed, reacts wildly, and loses his balance. His insides are overturned.

But Jesus promised, "If you are filled with light within, . . . then your face [the outside] will be radiant too, as though a floodlight is beamed upon you" (Luke 11:36, LB). Power comes from this inner light.

8. Take Charge of Your Feelings and They'll Work for You

You will maintain superpower if you stay on top of your feelings.

While in the bank one day, I picked up a brochure entitled "Your Key to Real Peace of Mind." Inside the cover was a startling answer—a safe deposit box!

We are bombarded with gimmicks that promise wholeness —pills, powder, and playthings—but many people are defeated by their feelings. As the pop tune puts it, "I'm singing the blues." The spiritual gets to the point: "I feel like a motherless child." A man spoke for many when he said, quoting Coleridge, "To be alone with my feelings is hell enough for me."

A lady insisted her life was at an end. "I'm completely tired of it," she confessed. "Tired! Tired! Tired!" She did not look old enough to be that tired; no one is. Although I realized I might be in an area where angels fear to tread, I asked her age. She remarked, "How old I feel or my age chronologically?" She was serious! She was thirty! Feelings pack a powerful punch.

I have been made aware of the awesome force of feelings through a personal experience. I want to share it in hopes you will be saved from the same dilemma or at least uncover the strength required to get through it.

Nineteen seventy was one of the toughest years of my life. I dipped to such a low valley that I am unable to fully describe it. It began when I looked at the huge undertakings of a young man. Things weren't going as they should, and when I reviewed my mistakes (what an experience that can be!), I assumed my church needed a pastor much greater than I (certainly the people were entitled to one!). I confronted all this without looking at the resources of a really big God who enables us and provides everything we need to do all we need to do!

Life, vitality, and enthusiasm drained from me. I felt pulled apart at the seams. Days were hard, and sleepless nights were almost intolerable. In the dark hours my heart hurt, and my mind annihilated my sense of judgment. During that year I stepped into my pulpit with fear and doubt.

Dread and dismay gnawed at my insides. No one on earth except my wife knew the shadows of those days. I am not sure she realized completely what was going on.

Depression does something to inner drive. My prayers seemed to get as far as the edge of my lips, then dropped into nothingness—unnoticed and unanswered. For months, I felt like a blob. At the end of my rope, I barely managed to hang on to life. At times I was sure that everyone and everything would be better off without me.

One day, I got a long-distance call from a close friend. "Dave," he asked, "is everything OK? I've had this unusual feeling about you." I was surprised at his call and the remarkable sense of perception which had come to him. Spiritual forces work among us, and even with our scientific, systematic, sophisticated learning, we are at a loss to explain how and why.

"I may not make it," I answered. "I feel hopelessly crushed! I need your prayers."

I closed my eyes and visualized him praying for me, and he did over the phone. We pictured ourselves together, kneeling, with a hand on each other's shoulder. His prayer must have come from far back in his bag of spiritual reserves, for it was timely and touching.

Although I sensed no instantaneous reassurance, an invisible power pulls us through such moments. It is like the little boy who had his kite so high it was invisible. A neighbor passing by stopped and looked up. "Young man, where's the kite?" he asked.

"Oh," replied the boy, "you can't see it."

"Is that so?" quipped the man. "Then how do you know it's there?"

Assuredly the little fellow shot back, "Because I feel the pull of it."

Although I did not feel the pull, God was still there.

I look back on that experience with tears and gladness. Never have I been through such canyons! Never have I learned such lessons! Since then, I appreciate people and other blessings—even the smallest blessings—in a way that I never anticipated. God has been so alive to me, so interesting, so close!

Feelings May Change!

A feeling of hope became a feeling of gloom for two college coeds. On graduation night, one said to the other, "Four long, hard, skimpy years and *whom* has it gotten us?"

Feelings can also be fickle. A man was madly in love with a beautiful woman. On her birthday, he decided to send twenty-five of the best roses money could buy—one rose for each year of her life—and a card of explanation. When the florist took the order, he thought, "This fellow is one of my finest customers. I'll really make him popular with his girl friend." The florist sent fifty roses! The man never knew what caused his fiancée to alter her feelings toward him!

But don't get alarmed when your feelings wane. That is part of their game.

If You Have No Feelings, Watch Out!

Without feelings you are unnatural and callous because you were given an inner sense to feel with your heart. Personality is a self-conscious being with powers of intellect, volition, and *emotion*. The mind feels; that is emotion. Without it, you have dried-up intellectualism, skulduggery, and pallid, raw, un-bearable living.

If Your Feelings Are Rampant, You Are in Trouble!

Rampant feelings take you into a world of make-believe, a fairy land. There is neither wisdom nor common sense to them. They have no solid roots.

Jesus had wild feelings in mind when he told the parable of the sower. Some seed fell on shallow soil; plants sprang up, all right, but they were withered by the hot sun. In explanation, the Master said, "The shallow, rocky soil represents the heart of a man who hears the message and receives it with real joy, but he doesn't have much depth in his life, and the seeds don't root very deeply, and after a while when trouble comes, . . . his enthusiasm fades, and he drops out" (Matt. 13:20–21, LB).

Runaway feelings are like unbridled horses. No one really knows where they will end up. You can be certain, though, that they will lead you on a merry-go-round and then leave you empty-handed.

Feelings May Let You Down!

Christianity never dodges the realities of life. It runs only one way—through them! When his feeling had him pinned down, the psalmist cried:

"Yet for a time, O Lord, you have tossed us aside in dis-honor, and have not helped us . . . You have actually fought against us and defeated us . . . You have treated us like sheep in a slaughter pen, . . . You sold us for a pittance. You valued us at nothing at all.

"Waken! Rouse yourself! Don't sleep, O Lord! Are we cast

off forever? Why do you look the other way? Why do you ignore our sorrows and oppression? We lie face downward in the dust.

"Rise up, O Lord, and come and help us" (Ps. 44:9–12, 23–26, LB).

God had thrown him to the side? Left him? Defeated him? Cared nothing for him any longer? God sleeping? Ignoring and rejecting him? Really, now! Of course not! But he *felt* like it! You too may have felt the same way because your feelings have let you down. Feelings boost life, but they are an inadequate base.

Alexis Carrel claimed that feeling and not reason leads a man to the height of his destiny. "The spirit rises by suffering and desire rather than by intellect, whose weight is too heavy, behind it. (Feeling) reduces itself to the essence of the soul which is love." Carrel wasn't an anti-intellectual but one of the wisest and most educated men of his time. Dr. Carrel also stated that intelligence is almost useless to those who possess nothing else. "The pure intellectual is an incomplete human being. He is unhappy because he is not capable of entering the world he understands." [1]

Feelings may be a beautiful helpmate to resourceful living, but they make a flimsy foundation. You need to stop being defeated by your feelings, and you may stop. It is possible for you to beat the agonizing feeling fall-out. Here are six ways.

Don't be afraid to question your feelings. The life of a minister brings him in contact with many different people. Much of the time, there is a need and he is asked to help. I recently encountered three interesting individuals who point out the wisdom of putting feelings on the question stand.

Glen, a nineteen-year-old university student, argued that feelings legalize, moralize, and authorize sexual relationships without the blessing of marriage. "If you feel for her," he said seriously, "really, deep inside, you have every right to show it sexually." I listened attentively as the young man empha-

sized his point; I knew him to have a strong religious upbring-
ing. "So I lived by this feeling for awhile," he continued. "I
felt I loved her."

Glen had to be away for ten weeks. When he returned, he
didn't have the same feeling for the girl. He came to the conclusion that he did not care enough to go on with her. Feelings had bested him.

He answered no when I asked if he had tested those feelings
before.

Every great feeling is willing to be questioned and tested!

For four years a beautiful twenty-eight-year-old housewife
carried on an affair with a friend. She didn't stop to question
her feelings although her conscience reminded her that she
was terribly wrong in what she was doing. She excused herself
by blaming her cold, indifferent, and unconcerned husband.

Feelings should be quizzed in many areas of life. I have a
forty-three-year-old friend who wanted to be in business for
himself. It was a life-long dream. Often Jim visualized himself
at the helm of his own firm. His aspirations were tremendous,
and he was sincere, but his impulses were not probed until his
floundering company landed on the rocks.

Some people live as if the only rule that counts is their own
feelings. What happens when you are depressed and despair of
life? In heaven's name, what logic is there to following your
impulse then? What happens when you feel like belting the
driver who swerves out in front of you? Can you possibly
justify the end to which such feelings may lead you? Of course
not!

Probe your feelings! Test your feelings! If feelings can't
take it, they aren't worth it! If they are worthwhile, they are
strong enough to stand it. Otherwise, they need to fall. You
can question your feelings by asking:

1. What is the motive behind this feeling?
2. What result may I expect from it?
3. Is it a good result?

4. If this feeling is transferred into reality, what will it do to others? (Great feelings do not make an island out of you nor do they hurt other people.)

5. What about God and this feeling? (Here is the highest testing.)

Condition your feelings. Fix an atmosphere which is likely to result in a particular outcome.

Most of us use thermostats to condition our houses to certain temperatures. In the cold of winter, a room can be conditioned to a cozy sixty-eight degrees. In the heat of summer, a room can be brought to a relaxing seventy-eight degrees. "OK," you wonder, "it works for a machine, but what about a man?"

A Texan won a gold watch for selling more cemetery lots than anybody else in America. He was actually enthusiastic about cemetery lots! For one thing, he knew that the market will never be exhausted! Everyone has to have one some time. And he believes Texas cemetery lots are the best money can buy. He says, "You can go to heaven faster from Texas than any other place in this world!" But the most enthusiasm was shown when he told what happened to him through spiritual power.

"I was full of unhealthy, unhappy things. I hated people, even myself. And I was awfully mixed up. A terrible inferiority complex, guilt, and a dullness toward life. Then I attended a meeting where a man told me what Jesus Christ could do in my life."

The Texan decided to read the New Testament. He began to understand it with his heart. Every morning, no matter how demanding his schedule, he would spend forty-five minutes with the Bible. "Then I would go out," he claims, "and have the time of my life all day long."

Feelings were conditioned! It does work for human beings! You can condition your feelings to defeat by holding to a defeating idea. "I can't" is a whopper! Soon, you will feel in the gutter. You can condition your feelings to success by holding to a successful idea. It helps you to the heights. Remember, feelings will be conditioned for good or bad; if not one, then the other. Which will it be?

Cultivate your feelings. Feelings do not just happen! They are the yield of an input, and the crop depends on cultivation.

As a young man, I began my ministry on the high plains of West Texas. That wind-whipped dustbowl of the Great Depression has been transformed into some of the most productive farm land in the country. Miles and miles of endless wheat fields blow in the breeze; the earth appears to be heaving rhythmically like swells in a great ocean.

The farmers in my congregation knew what it meant to cultivate crops. First, if they were smart, they released their hopes and soil to God. Then they prepared the ground for planting. After that, they seeded it, burying the grain a few inches into the earth. Then, the tender, new crop required care: plowing, watering, and spraying to defy hungry insects. The outcome depended on cultivation.

Since you become your deepest and tenacious feelings, it is imperative to cultivate them with cheerful, never-dying, success ingredients. Those feelings will grow; they will leap forward to maturity, and you will too. You will be amazed at your happiness.

Control your feelings. When you cultivate your feelings with the proper ingredients, control is no longer an insurmountable problem. One of the most well-loved stories in the Bible concerns Jesus and his great temptation (Luke 4). The Galilean would have fallen to temptation had his feelings not been controlled.

He was hungry, and hunger drives people to extremes. Once there was a tribe of natives which missionaries converted to Christ. They were taught in mission schools and trained by dedicated workers; yet in a famine they killed one another for food.

Christ was offered fame. You have felt the urge to become famous, haven't you? You probably imagined your name in bright lights. For a moment, the thought of stardom sent chills down your spine. Even newspapers were resplendent with bold headlines of your fantastic achievements. You envisioned yourself in the president's chair or as chairman of the board, his wife, the boss, the leadman, or the supervisor. Perhaps the most humbling experience of your life came when you finally realized that you may be winding up a notch or two under the bright lights. A man said to me, "Dave, at age forty-eight I am at the most frustrating time of my life. I see that I will probably never be president of the company which has twenty-five years of my life."

Jesus did the most wonderful thing: He put fame on another plane. "We must worship God, and him alone." The truest attainment of fame comes when who you are as a person and what you have outlive the things in life.

God: You may have nothing else, but when you have him, you are famous.

Dignity: Anyone who holds his or her head up from a courageous heart is famous.

Hope: Everyone who believes in his or her heart that life is worth living all the days of life is famous.

The last temptation had to do with invincibility. There is no sense to it at all! Uncontrolled feelings will tempt you to deify self. They make you cocky and arrogant.

Basically the matter of control is a question of *who* or *what* is boss within you. Feelings? No wonder you have a fallout! A *what* is in charge. Are you in charge? Then you have a fall-in. Feelings fall into place, for a *who* is in charge.

Channel your feelings. You may be a reservoir or a channel. One is a container; the other is a conductor. If your life is self-contained, you suffer from pent-up feelings. Often these feelings become anxiety, and sooner or later, the dam will break! If your life is a conductor, it flows. Feelings are channeled in creative ways. You take your feelings, whatever they are, and convert them into a funnel of enrichment, remembering that impression without expression causes depression.

Both up and down feelings can be turned into a conduit of usefulness because you can always identify with others since they have similar feelings. (The similarity is amazing.) Sometimes they feel up; sometimes you feel up, therefore, you help them. Sometimes they feel down; sometimes you feel down and you're honest about it, therefore, you can help them.

As a result, you are awakened to a better, happier, overcoming life. You dedicate yourself to do it. You sense it, and you do it. Feeling has become a mighty channel.

A young man is aroused to give his life to a high calling. He perceives the touch of God on him, and he responds, "Here am I, Lord. Yours!" His feeling has become a channel.

You are moved by the needs of people. You are stimulated to support a worthy endeavor. You are quickened to involve yourself in a people-lifting project. There is a keen warmth in you to do it; a fervent spirit motivates you, and you begin. Feeling has become a channel. Until feeling becomes a channel, life is a cage! Only then does feeling become a declaration of the depths.

Consecrate your feelings. Consecration takes feelings to the core of life and attaches them to faith. When they stem from honest faith, the steps we have discussed become reality. They find their ultimate connection and their authentic fulfillment in faith.

The thermostat regulates the temperature, but the best the thermometer can do is register the temperature! Feeling is a thermometer; it reveals. Faith is a thermostat; it manages.

Dr. T. R. Glover, the renowned historian, says that Marcus Aurelius did not believe enough to be great. Perhaps you are not believing enough to experience the steps which beat your feeling fallout and bring you to victory! How much faith does it?

Jesus spoke of faith even as small as a grain of mustard seed, a microscopic entity. But the seed contains all the potential for a full-grown plant. Faith to begin does not need to be large, but it must be all faith—pure and genuine. The possibilities in even a little faith are more comprehensive than you have ever thought!

Faith gets to the heart of things. Many people are depending on a pill. Faith is not a pill. Faith portends the highest power! It consummates, integrates, and conglomerates life into fullest meaning. Faith is the answer, not an anesthetic!

Dell and Betty Lamm are friends of mine. At lunch one day, I asked Dell how he became a key man in the church renewal ministry started by Dr. E. Stanley Jones. "OK," he answered, "you asked for it. Twelve years ago I was at the bottom of life. My business was wrecked. Income skidded to nothing. I drank heavily. My marriage was on the rocks, and my feelings were defeating me. Our son had left home, and we hadn't heard from him since he walked out. Betty suggested that before we throw in the towel we see another marriage counselor. But I reminded her that we'd been to psychologists before. Nevertheless I consented to go." Unknown to them, the counselor was a Christian.

Dell was asked, "What is a Christian?"

That startled him. He answered, "Somebody who goes to church on Sunday and keeps his nose clean." He told me that he had taught a Sunday school class at one time even though he didn't know much about the Bible or Christianity. The counselor suggested that a Christian opens himself to Jesus Christ by whom he is empowered to live a transforming and overcoming existence. "I never thought of it like that," Dell recalled.

Their counselor felt that Dell and Betty could continue their weekly sessions but that ultimate power for a happy marriage and right relationships would come only through an honest commitment to Jesus Christ, and he told them so. Dell said,

"Our counselor asked if we had ever been to one of E. Stanley Jones's ashrams [a retreat]. We indicated that we hadn't. Quickly, he advised us to go to one scheduled to begin nearby in a few days." Dell and Betty debated and finally agreed to attend the weeklong retreat.

"While there Dr. Jones prayed for us and with us. We decided to make an honest commitment to God, as best we knew how. Do you know what we experienced? A sense of forgiveness of our sins and a release from the tensions, anxieties, and resentments we had clung to for a long time—especially toward our son who had hurt us badly. Through faith, Jesus Christ became a living power in our lives.

"Afterwards, we began to grow personally and to build a solid, loving, new relationship with each other. We joined a church and began to serve the Lord. Incidentally, business is booming again. Can you beat that? The more we give of ourselves, the more we really have—for ourselves and others."

These two people discovered and used the power. Dell and Betty are singled out for the heights and so are you! If you are willing to start as an overcomer, it can happen to you! You can take charge of your feelings!

9. Get the Team Spirit and Do Away with Loneliness

You will enjoy a truly great power if you begin to practice positive interdependence.

When a person unearths something that profoundly affects him, he wants to share it. I have made a discovery that has empowered me, and I want to share it. It has changed my way of living, led me to a new approach to tasks, and lifted me to a higher level of efficiency.

The secret lies in the *team* spirit, a requirement for overcomers. *Team* means everything that makes up you, spirit and body, all of you working in harmony.

A man who sounded really desperate called my office and asked to see me. I invited him over immediately. The first time I saw him, he appeared to be battling with himself. A struggle marked his pale face. His conscience balked at his actions; his mind squabbled with the way he treated his body. His body reacted to his feelings. His spirit longed for a higher, better way; it would not tolerate mediocrity. The difficulty was that he didn't have the team spirit *in* himself.

A new happiness and inner togetherness began when the team spirit came to all areas in his life. They stopped warring with one another and formed a beautiful squad—all striving for the same goal. He began to realize that every life requires a flow of unity. Only then can a person experience his or her greatest possibilities.

Team also refers to all of *us* working on the team. In this sense *team* is a numerical concept, involving more than one human being—wife, husband, children (wouldn't it be great to have the team spirit in the family?), associates, colleagues, employees. This team has sustaining and stabilizing power.

Joe, a man of thirty-seven, had once been an effusive, confident individual. In a few years he had achieved a level of success few people attain in a lifetime. Now he was shaken to the core. Everything looked bad—dreams torpedoed, hopes dashed, life sliding to the bottom. He began to lose interest in people, and he degenerated physically. He became weak and susceptible to illnesses. "Never had so many sniffles and sneezes in my life," he recounted.

Tiredness shadowed him morning, noon, and night. Life was dim; the days were dreary; getting up was difficult; it was hard to go to sleep, and it was hard to stay asleep.

Oliver Wendell Holmes said that enthusiasm for something makes life worth looking at, but Joe had lost that enthusiasm. The future was a dreaded nightmare; the past, a holocaust; and the present, a cheap existence. "More than once I thought death was the best way out," he said.

What kept him going? "My wife and God," he said. There is the *us* team at work. He told me that at times he was not sure God still loved him. "At least, I didn't feel he did, but I was so ingrained by that love I couldn't get away from it.

"My wife understood me more than ever. She was amazing! She stood under me emotionally and held me up. She wouldn't let me go. 'Honey,' she'd say, 'you have too much to give. I won't let you quit [living]. I love you, and we'll pull through. Things will work out.' "

Most life-builders—those who forge ahead—have gone through similar experiences. They have been helped greatly by the *us* team. Remember, to be an overcomer, you don't have to be an expert in everything.

The team spirit makes the overcomer through the team. The team opens to you the services of an expert. A man once explained to me that an expert is one who can hit the bullseye without shooting the bull. The story is told that Henry Ford was charged with ineptness. "You don't know the first thing about engineering and mechanics," claimed his accusers.

"Maybe so," the wise man replied, "but by pressing these buttons I can summon a hundred different men who do." The secret is to keep experts available.

Preserve Your Nerves Through the Team Spirit

It is a nerve-wracking job to try to do everything yourself. A young man found himself head of a fast-growing manufacturing company. Mark, and his wife, Peggy, worked hard. They started from scratch, but they had energy, enthusiasm, and stamina, and they were determined. In a few years, business was incredibly good, and to meet the schedules, Mark began working night and day, seven days a week. His product filled a great need in industry. The orders came in rapidly as word about him got around.

Furthermore, he felt he had to tend personally to many business details. It was only a matter of time until Peggy called. "Reverend, Mark is cracking up." The team spirit would have saved him an awful experience. The lesson came the hard way.

Wear and tear, pills, worry, heartache, sleepless nights, and fitful days are no way to carry on the business of living! Instead, look forward to each day with confidence that success awaits you.

The team spirit will help. Feeling alone, an older friend said that the first thing he does after he wakes up each morning is read the obituary column in the paper. If he is not listed there, he goes ahead and eats breakfast.

In contrast, one of the wonderful possibilities in life is to actually look forward to each day, to have confidence within that promises success through anything that comes. Larry, a traveling salesman, wrote:

"When I began working as a pharmaceutical salesman, I

was bursting with energy. Customers were persons to me. I took the time to deal with them on a human-to-human basis. Sales increased each year. [In fact, Larry became the leading representative in the Western states for his company.] But in five or six years, things started to drop. I began to slack off; the time came when I didn't care about the people. Sales plunged. Family problems began to overwhelm me. As for life, my interest in it dropped a few notches everyday. Eventually I started wondering if I had any future."

On a trip to San Diego, he stayed overnight. On the dresser of his hotel room was a copy of *Spiritual Starters for a Successful Day,* a booklet I wrote that outlines some basic spiritual principles which can help develop an inner confidence that success awaits you every day. The key, of course, is to give yourself as you are and as completely as you know to Jesus Christ, as much as you understand him.

Larry said, "I thumbed through the booklet, and I asked myself, 'Does this really work?' I couldn't answer at that time because I hadn't tried it. But I felt that I had nothing to lose and everything to gain by giving it an honest try."

Larry said he read the booklet a second time and the Bible verses about confidence and courage began to work deep in his soul. He wrote, "I experienced a sensation never before known to me—although I had been considered a religious fellow. The feeling came over me that I should kneel there in the hotel room and give myself, like you say, just as I am and as completely as I know to Jesus Christ, as much as I understand him. I did! Man, what a different person I've been ever since then, and by applying the spiritual principles of faith, I have gained a sense of confidence that you wouldn't believe. God is doing this to me."

There is no need to face the day without confidence. There is no problem so big that it should push aside confidence and courage. Success awaits. It is there for *you.* What you need is the team spirit.

The Team Spirit Introduces an Interdependence
Which Frees You to Positive Independence

Our society has been blessed by a philosophy which emphasizes rugged individualism. The pilgrims, pioneers, and settlers had to be self-reliant. It was a question of survive or sink. Each of us is responsible for clearing new frontiers—yes, even in our day—and many frontiers await our attention! But when self-reliance gets beyond interdependence, it becomes cocky self-reference. What is intended to make us strong then makes us hard. What is designed to anchor the fiber of human nature against the knocks of defeat and setbacks degenerates into isolationism. Arrogance sidesteps warm human relationships as though they were a sign of weakness and timidity.

Jesus spoke of a rich man who became an arrogant fool. "I will tear down my barns and I will build bigger barns. I . . . I . . . I" (see Luke 12:18).

"Mrs. Self-Dependence" comes to mind. "I don't want to bother anyone," she said. "In fact, I'm sure I am imposing on you by coming here." A young, potentially outstanding person, she felt at the end of her rope.

"Have you ever asked anyone to help you?" I asked.

"No! No! Of course not!"

Life had halted, and she looked forsaken. Up to that time, she had not understood the power and blessings of positive independence through interdependence. Until you allow others to help you as they can, you are not really independent. You are a slave cooped up within yourself, a shell, a cage. You are missing more of life than you think. Thomas á Kempis said that no one is so sufficient as to never need assistance. Wordsworth spoke of two requirements for character and success which go together: humble dependence on God and manly reliance on self. Remember, we are made to help each other. It is a wonderful sign of humanity. Until we help others, we are not living up to our possibilities. We need the help others can provide. Until we permit others to help us, we are shielding ourselves from their possibilities, and we are claiming that we do not need anyone—a lie!

Seneca, the Roman philosopher, said, "All my life I have been seeking to climb out of this pit, and I can't do it. I never will, unless a hand is let down to me to draw me up." Like everyone else, Seneca could go ahead only by the assistance of people.

Given a chance, the team spirit reinforces, enlightens, extends, expands, enables, expresses, and impresses you. The team spirit is a necessity in every life, but how do you get it? Both "all of *you*" and "all of *us*" may be found in the following ways.

Share yourself. The first time some followers of Jesus asked who is the greatest in the kingdom of heaven, the Master made it clear that great people become as little children.

The children in my neighborhood (and there are many) seem most willing to share communicable diseases and mother's age. At least they are willing to share! A boy who lives nearby made the mistake of coming outside with a heaping ice cream cone. Within seconds, playmates swarmed around him like hungry flies, each wanting a lick. The boy shared until he had left only the remnants of a chewed-up cone and a few drops of melted chocolate dripping from his hand.

A child's natural inclination to share is part of what Jesus meant about our becoming as little children. We need to give spontaneously of who and what we are.

Sharing changes you and others through you. A man sat in my office and admitted candidly, "There is not a single reason for me to live. I don't have a purpose and haven't had for a long time. So it is easier for me to die than go on living."

"You don't believe your life is worth living," I said. "Well, I'm sure it can be, and until you believe it, I'll believe for you. OK?" The man broke down, promising he would make no more attempts on his life until God had a chance to remake him.

Faith is a wonderful spirit to share in times like these. Sometimes it will involve a *transfer* of faith. "Until you believe (can believe for yourself), I'll believe for you."

Some friends brought a paralyzed man to Jesus. Apparently, the past had buckled him under. He was physically helpless and emotionally whipped. "Seeing their faith, Jesus said to the man, 'My friend, your sins are forgiven! . . . Pick up your stretcher and go on home'" (Luke 5:18–20, 24, LB).

Such a faith releases fantastic power! You can do more, reach higher, live taller, go farther than you have imagined. Faith guarantees it. Sharing it does something for you and for those with whom you share.

Serve. One time the Galilean was questioned about who is great, and he replied that great people become servants. Amazingly the greatest person has a high estimate of himself, or he would not serve. He has a serving mentality, and that is smart!

1. He finds a need and fills it with his life. (This is a must for thinking people.)
2. He does it from the heart. (Love is the force).
3. He makes service the first line, the priority. (Help is his objective.)
4. He lets all other returns be what they must be—results. (And they are remarkable.)

An insurance salesman in my church said that he is *not* primarily out for the dollar. "I am more concerned with rendering a true service," he said. "I advise my clients as to their *needs* as I see them based on my knowledge of their situation. Then I try to meet those needs. If I am unable to do it, I refer them to somebody who can." It isn't surprising that he has been a member of the Million Dollar Roundtable every year he has been in the insurance business! At the time I write this chapter, it is near the end of January and he has already

passed the one million dollar mark for 1977. People who
render the service selflessly receive the rewards the service
draws out of people.

Another member of my congregation was a leading carpet
salesman in his company. "I have one guiding principle in all
of my contracts," he said. "I give the customer an honest
service. Couples with children used to come in my store and
insist on white carpet. In those days, white carpet was a status
symbol! I'd point out the value of another color carpet because growing children have a way of keeping white carpet a
sickening brown color. One of ten such couples would walk
out without buying. The four who agreed with me and bought
another carpet remembered the service I try to provide and
influenced dozens of more customers to see me for their carpet
needs.

Such individuals have a sense of respect, accomplishment,
and helpfulness inside. Nothing can substitute for that! In the
case of the two men I have mentioned, there was professional
recognition.

Victory always comes in *cans,* failure in *can'ts.* You *can*
give yourself in meaningful service. You've given yourself to
God when you receive forgiveness; so you are most able to
give to others. You have something to give. Others need you.
Every service is important. As Robert Browning said, "All
service ranks the same with God." Beran Wolfe stated that
"no one has learned the meaning of life until he has surrendered his ego to the service of his fellow men." And in the
Chicago Daily News, "He who lives for self and self alone is
a successful failure." I tried to emphasize this in *Discoveries
for Peaceful Living* by saying that deed meeting need never
goes out of style. Service is the spirit. There is room at the top
for you. You're always ahead when you serve—not behind.

Service makes a person great. "If any man serves me, the
Father will honor him." Those are familiar words from the
Bible (John 12:26, RSV). R. G. LeTourneau, the famous in-

dustrialist, got the idea across in his inimitable way. Often he remarked that it pays to serve the Lord, but don't serve the Lord because it pays. If you serve the Lord only because it pays, it may not pay. The unadulterated "serve for pay" person has mixed-up and miscalculated motivation.

Sacrifice. This really is not a harsh word when you understand what it means and how much it can add to life. Sacrifice means giving yourself to something bigger than yourself which always deserves and demands a notch more.

But too many of us have the idea of the Russian who was being examined for party membership. "If you had one million dollars," queried the Communists, "would you give half to the party?"

"Of course!"

"If you had ten thousand acres of rich land, would you give half to the party?"

"A ridiculous question! You know I would!"

"If you had two pair of pants, would you give one to the party?"

"No."

"No? Why not?"

"I have two pair of pants." [1]

Most of us do not really sacrifice enough. Usually we are not stimulated as much as our capabilities can take. Most of us never utilize more than 10 percent of our possibilities. It is rather pathetic that 90 percent of what we might contribute to the good of mankind is wasted in a day which needs the best, highest, and most we have to offer.

We are not urged enough. Sometimes we have our values out of order. For example, many people have sacrificed themselves—their bodies, faith, health, worship, family, and friends—on the altar of "things." But the truth is, things are not big enough to hold on to you! They are not deserving or demanding enough! They are just big enough to break you if you have them out of perspective!

Get your strength from the Scriptures. One of the most prominent businessmen in the Southern states told me that he gets ideas from the Bible by which to solve the knottiest business problems. He finds suggestions that help him improve methods of management and which give him guidance for day-to-day operations of his manufacturing company. He discovers power to apply Christian principles to company life and the way to bring out the possibilities in his employees. "Everyone gains from it," he said.

Furthermore, the Bible tells about the greatest team member you may have—Jesus Christ. It points out his availability now, the way to him, and his program for a successful life.

Your day will become much more meaningful when you start it with the Bible. I know a man who invests thirty minutes in Bible reading every morning and another thirty minutes for meditation, prayer, and evaluation. Yes, his schedule is so tight that it is almost unbelievable. "Life has never been the same since I became serious about this," he says.

Through this unusual team Book—the Bible—you find insight for personal problem-solving and family unity and power for the present and hope for the future. You may be released to the life for which the inner self yearns. Try it!

Add to your strength by regular worship in the sanctuary. The dictionary speaks of a sanctuary as both a sacred place and an asylum. Either one may have something to do with sanity.

After going through a traumatic crisis, a church member said, "Were it not for the friends in my church, the fellowship, and the power in worship which flows from here every week, I believe I would have lost my mind."

Possibly you need to give some serious thought to the salutary effect church membership and churchgoing can have on your health. What if the risk of fatal heart disease for those who attend church infrequently were nearly twice as high as for those who attend once a week or more? What if there were a connection between nervous disorders, mental illness, cancer, cirrhosis, tuberculosis, and respiratory illnesses and church attendance?

Such matters are not to be joked off, for they reflect on the dynamic influence the church may have on your life.

The church doing its job is a power and light company, a center of spiritual life, a center of creative living, a Christian action group. The church is for purposes of restoration, rejuvenation, rededication, and rehabilitation.

Besides fellowship, there are three reasons every believer should become an active church member.

1. The church needs you because the church may become better and God can use you to better it.
2. You need the church because you may become a fuller, happier person and God can use the church to help you do it.
3. You need to reinforce the church for the good the church stands for.

After traveling around the world touring every kind of benevolent work conceivable, a man said he never saw a single hospital, sanitarium, mission, or orphanage sponsored by a society of atheists or agnostics! Today behind the Iron Curtain, communism represses and supresses Christians, forbidding the church to gather. In 1933, Hitler swore that the church was rotten to the core and that within a few months he would close every church door in Germany.

Now do you see why I am an enthusiastic salesman for active membership? Do you understand the urgency with which I encourage active membership? Why I relentlessly and joyfully invite you to show your faith and join the church? To me, it is not a matter to delay.

The team spirit will make a wonderful difference in your life! As a matter of fact, it will do wonders for your family and your business. Demonstrate a team spirit on your job, and you may well open the door to promotions. Surprise your boss with a new team spirit. He will probably never get over it.

Every team needs a strong, well-qualified knowledgeable leader. What happens to the football team who has no leader? A professional team accustomed to winning was taking a solid beating. The commentator who used to be with the losing team explained, "Well, they don't have a leader today. The spirit is missing."

As a boy, my friends and I planned a three-day hike through some treacherous mountains in Texas. Before the idea went too far, our parents wanted to know who the guide was and if he knew the way through the mountains.

Your team requires a leader. God is the best! The confidence of his nearness each day is the best tonic for loneliness available. With him in charge of your team, you have at your fingertips the power to power you through life.

10. Fill Up with Faith
and Fade Out Your Fear

*You will get power extraordinary if you use faith
to conquer your fears.*

Fear, your number one enemy, keeps you from an overcoming life because fear stifles positive expression and over-
whelms with deadly pessimism. Fear weakens the will, curses
courage, erodes effort, and diminishes drive. It causes worry,
tension, panic, mismanagement, tiredness, sickness, and even
death.

Research at the University of New Mexico demonstrated
that fear impairs vision. Exhaustive studies at the University
of Colorado proved that fear interferes with the ability to
reason and think. Mental apparatus may work faster but not
as efficiently. Quality of thinking declines noticeably. What
do people fear most?

Loss

The fear of loss cut one man's inheritance from three million
dollars to five hundred thousand dollars. He married a very
wealthy, beautiful young woman. Even though they seemed
madly in love, he was always afraid his wife would leave him
for another man. To prevent that, he decided to have lots of
children. At least, the children would make divorce more difficult, he reasoned.

The wife had no intentions of leaving him, but when she
became aware of his scheme, she felt he ought to pay for his
fear. With her lawyer, she devised a plan whereby, at her
death, her fearful husband would receive a share of her estate
equal to each child's share. The more children, the smaller his

share! At last count, the father had cut his inheritance to half a million dollars.

People are afraid to lose because they want to hold on to what they have—a classic mistake. Real freedom is attained when you're willing to lose everything. Abundant life begins when you could (not necessarily do) lose everything and go on living. Scripture states that one who loses life will find it. Willingness, not actual loss, is the secret.

Openness

To live in secret is to live in defeat; yet the thought of exposure shell shocks some of us. The corner bar, where shared secrets may or may not be repeated, is a prime example of man's need to live in the open. In *Dare to Live Now,* Bruce Larson claims that the "neighborhood bar is an imitation, dispensing liquor instead of grace, escape instead of reality, but it is an accepting and inclusive fellowship."

He continues, "You can tell people secrets and they usually don't tell others or even want to. The bar flourishes, not because people are alcoholics, but because God has put into the human heart the desire to know and be known, to love and be loved, and so many seek a counterfeit at the price of a few beers." [1]

A person is free to the extent that he or she is willing to be known.

Vulnerability

Some people are handcuffed by feeling they have to be right all the time; they think they can never be wrong. Since perfection is their god, they feel threatened when their position is questioned. Someone who represents an improvement upsets their apple cart.

I am acquainted with a woman who is quick to broadcast

her ideas but takes offense when anyone questions them or suggests modification. In exasperation one day she told me, "I've been thinking about my feelings when others in the group don't agree completely with what I say. Through prayer I've come to the conclusion that I'm basically afraid to be vulnerable."

I asked, "And what are you going to do about it?"

Thoughtfully she answered, "Let God change my attitude. Also I will try to keep in mind the value of others' ideas and that we're all human."

She made a perceptive observation, for all people are imperfect. The imperfection of those who are afraid to be vulnerable grows like a cancer. Their lives become infected. It isn't a catastrophe to be imperfect, but it's destructive to be afraid to admit it.

Failure

Shakespeare said, "We lose the good we oft might win by fearing to attempt." The fear of failure produces failure, and it will prevent a person from even trying.

A friend of mine went through a period in his life when he was afraid of failure. Then he came across some words which brought him to his senses: "I'd rather attempt to do something great and fail, than attempt to do nothing and succeed."

What pride is there in succeeding at nothing? What hope is generated? What faith is fired up? What lives are changed? What persons are touched? What generation is moved higher? What good is accomplished? Only those who dare to try become fruitful. Great results require an investment—effort.

The person who succumbs to the fear of failure loses what he has (see Luke 19:20–21). By trying, you risk failure; you can be shot down only when you're standing up.

Remember, a worm should be the only thing that can't fall down. It is no dishonor to fall; it is a dishonor to stay down moaning and groaning. It is human to fail! Failure is never complete unless you pamper it and stick to it. There is certainly nothing glorious about failure, but the worst thing about failure is the fear of it.

Comparison

Those afraid of comparison keep asking themselves, "Do I match up to ____?" "I've got to have one because ____ has one" is the result.

A young man's life was wrecked by this fear. His father, a prominent man in his vocation and community, had worked his way to the top from a humble background and beginning. Early in the young man's life, he began to fear comparison. He was doing poorly in school even though he had the ability to do quite well.

Finally, a counselor talked to him. Through tests, the counselor determined that the young man was so conscious of his dad's prominence that he believed he had to be perfect. In any situation where he couldn't be perfect, he gave up. He wouldn't even try. Since even the best of persons have imperfections, it isn't surprising that the young man gave up more often than not.

Each of us is a person in his or her own right and needn't fear comparison with anyone else. We are responsible to be all that God wants us to be—nothing more and nothing less.

Contradiction

The fear of contradiction expresses itself in a hesitation to make thoughts and feelings known. Consciously or unconsciously, you don't want to make contradiction a possibility; so you keep nice and quiet in your own little world. There's no risk that way. Someone asks what you think and you shy away from a straight-from-the-shoulders reply. Maybe you talk, but you don't say anything. Perhaps you ramble to fill time and space, or you turn to someone else and ask, "What do you think?"

The New

Fear of the new keeps people old. *Never* and *always* are sacred words to a person who is afraid of innovation.

"I (or we) *never* did it that way before."

"I've (we've) *always* done it this way and *always* will!"

Such a fear will bankrupt a person or an enterprise.

Past

To fear the past is destructive and is manifest in a disrespect for heritage, roots, and experience. Such a fear produces constant instability. Change at all costs is worshiped.

Success

Believe it or not, many people fear success. I heard a businessman give the following formula for success: Create a product that costs one dollar to make, sells for five dollars, and is habit-forming. Maybe we need a fresh look at the meaning and value of success.

The best measure of success is character, not achievement. The other day, a man boasted, "I've got a blankety-blank sixty-thousand-dollar house and a six-figure bank balance. I couldn't care less about the stock market nowadays. Reverend, looks like I've made a blankety-blank good success, wouldn't you say?" He could be congratulated on his beautiful house, the enviable bank balance, and his independence from topsy-turvy economic conditions. But I would not say he is a success. Anyone who loves sincerely, laughs often, and lives happily is a success.

"Add goodness to your faith; to your goodness add knowledge; to your knowledge add self-control; to your self-control add endurance; to your endurance add godliness; to your godliness add brotherly love; and to your brotherly love add love. These are the qualities you need [most], and if you have them in abundance they will make you active and effective" (2 Pet. 1:5–8, TEV).

You've heard that God calls you to be faithful, not successful. God's will is not that you achieve a goal but that you attempt it; that the Lord holds you accountable for obedience, not success; that he judges you by your efforts, not by your accomplishments. There is truth to such statements, but they often become excuses for failure. They litter the pathway to mediocrity, halfway living, and a blah life-experience.

God calls you to your highest! You can expect victory, and success! Furthermore, you can expect release from the fear of success.

People

The fear of people leads a person to shun social contact and involvement. "I've been hurt by people," you explain, "so I'm avoiding them." Of course, you have been hurt by people. That is the price for being human.

Some people fear other people who aren't "on their level" or "in their circle." They are afraid of people who are a different color and who speak a different language. Such fear keeps our world on the brink of catastrophe, our cities and communities tense, and our society uptight. This fear produces the idea that we must protect "our" kind from "their" kind.

How unlike the experience John Oxenham refers to his hymn:

> In Christ there is no East or West,
> In Him no South or North;

But one great fellowship of love
Throughout the whole wide earth.[2]

Fear of people torpedoes relationships because it breeds suspicion and distrust.

"Supposed" Facts

Most fear, like worry, stems from what you think will happen. Take King Herod, for example. He feared what people *might* do (see Matt. 14:5). He was afraid of what a young woman *might* say (see Matt. 14:9). Supposed fear—brought on by what you think has happened, is happening, or will happen—is a degenerating emotion.

In this connection, Henry Van Dyke said, "Men are disturbed not by the thing that happens, but by what they *think* happens." [3] Some interesting experiments clarified this matter of supposed fear.

Under clinical direction in sunny Los Angeles, a man was hypnotized and told that he was at the North Pole. Soon he began to shiver and demonstrate symptoms of being extremely cold. He even developed goose pimples! Some college students were asked to suppose that one hand was submerged in ice cold water when, in fact, the hand was resting on a walnut table in very warm surroundings. The thermometer used for the experiment recorded a definite drop in temperature in the treated hand.

What does all this mean? The nervous system and emotion-center do not distinguish, by themselves, between the real and the supposed. One can suppose strongly enough to bring the supposed into emotional and physiological reality. Emotionally, you get frantic and panicky. Physically, without doing a lick of work, you (through the amazing powers of "suppose") become tired, pooped, energyless, fidgety, fatigued, tension-ridden, pain-riddled, and headached into defeat.

Wrote a distinguished doctor, Maxwell Maltz, "[The human nervous system] reacts proportionately to what one thinks or imagines to be true and real." [4]

Dr. William Standish Reed of the American Board of Surgery authored a question-and-answer magazine column. One lady wrote in: "I have had a cancer removed in which a large skin graft was used and no x-ray. What is my hope with this condition? Must I face a possible recurrence?" Dr. Reed gave an elaborate medical reply, then added another observation of considerable importance:

The fear of recurrence can, in itself, produce the recurrence. Thoughts are living things with the force of overt acts. By fear, even subconscious, we can produce abnormalities in our body.

How potent is "supposed" fear! Lamentably, man's greatest fears spring from what he supposes.

Yourself

A personable, handsome, clean-cut, all-American, twenty-two-year-old young man was afraid of himself. Duane graduated from a highly respected church-affiliated college and, one week later, robbed a bank. In the process, he put 22-caliber bullets in the heads of four employees as they lay face down on the floor.

Before snuffing out his life, a brilliant forty-one-year-old insurance executive wrote: "I cannot live with myself any longer."

The last words of a young housewife and appreciated mother in Houston, Texas, read: "I don't have the ability to maintain a good home." An eighteen-year-old lad said: "I don't fit in."

Overcoming Fear

These all-star fears look huge, but they are surmountable through a nine-step treatment.

1. As much as possible, find out what you fear. How can you handle a blur? What can you do about what you don't know? Overcoming an unknown fear can be like a boxer fighting an invisible, unknown opponent—jabbing at the air. To find out what you fear, write down on a sheet of paper what you think you fear. Then put those fears in order of importance, as you see them.

2. Face your fears honestly. Like realities, fears have to be confronted.

One day I was on a plane headed for Florida. Over the Southern states, close-to-the-ground storms and floods were visible. For about thirty minutes, the big jet upped and downed with alarming regularity. Sitting next to me was a Dutchman from Hebron, Indiana, with whom I had talked for an hour or so. Unconsciously, I placed my hands in what must have been a prayerlike position. My fingers were together in A-frame style, resting against my mouth. Dutch looked at me and said, "Reverend, is that any indication of what we ought to be doing or of what's ahead?"

Suddenly, I noticed my hands and realized what he referred to. I answered, "It wouldn't hurt."

He said, "I don't know about you, but this scares me."

That was an honest confrontation with fear. When you face fears honestly, you'll discover what millions have: Standing up to fear scissors it down, or strengthens you, or both. At any rate, you uncover more power to deal with it.

"Yes," you should say, "I'm afraid of (*name it*)."

3. Recognize fear for what it is—a defeating emotion that can be overcome! It is usually a falsehood or, at least, a mismanagement of the truth. When you push the panic button, fear blows up into gigantic proportions. Size up your fears, and you'll size them down to size.

4. *Tackle your fears step by step.* You didn't acquire fear or fears all at once. You accumulated them piecemeal; so take charge of your fears individually and eliminate them.

5. *Do what you fear,* using God-given sense in light of what the fear is. Attacking fear directly brings out the cowardice in fear. This technique was illustrated to me while we were returning home from vacation.

We stayed overnight in a hotel at Casa Grande, Arizona. The swimming pool was large and well-designed with a nice diving board. I watched a girl about twelve or thirteen years old as she walked slowly to the end of the board and looked down at the water. Timidly, she bounced on the board, stopped, and backed away. Again she walked to the edge and bounced several times. "I don't know," she mumbled. For the second time she backed away.

An older brother who was already in the pool yelled, "Come on, Susan, it's great."

She replied, "I've never dived from this board. It scares me."

"Go ahead," brother urged. "It won't hurt you."

Timidly she walked to the end of the board, stood for a minute, and said, "There's only one way to overcome this fear." And she dived in. Before long she had dived dozens of times. Of course, by doing what she feared, Susan overcame the fear.

6. *Change your performance.* Upgrade it.

A man was afraid of losing his job as manager because sales in his department were down 6 percent when all other departments in his company were up 8 percent. At a management meeting, he felt the squeeze as another, aggressive department head slyly suggested that his department be expanded to include the man's department which was down in sales. The manager called his staff together to evaluate the past year and outline goals for the next twelve months, and he challenged them. The results were amazing. Sales began to climb as employees changed their performance, and they did away with the fear of losing their jobs.

7. *Fill fear-space with purpose.* "Shall I say, 'Father, do not let this hour come upon me?' But that is why I came, . . . Father, bring glory to your name," said Jesus (John 12:27–28, TEV).

Some time ago, the American Medical Association shocked millions of us with the report that middle age begins at twenty-five and continues through sixty-five. A demolishing concept for many under age forty! According to the report, the biggest problem in these middle years is alchoholism. Two reasons were given.

First, a watered-down or complete lack of a sense of identity. "Who am I—really?" Second, "Why am I?" What's my purpose here?

As Jesus pointed out, your mind will be dominated by something—fear unless you have a purpose big enough to live for (see Matt. 12:43–45). You can go through anything when a purpose great enough is deep enough in your will and thoughts (see John 12:23–24).

8. *When you sense fear approaching, fill your mind with inspiring, courage-reinforcing thoughts.* Dr. Paul White, the famous heart specialist, illustrated the power of inspirational thoughts in the *Annals of Internal Medicine.* A surgeon performed an operation on a man to remove cancer. A few days after surgery, the doctor said the patient was going to die. Medically, he was safe in making the prognosis, but he failed to take into account Henry's optimism.

"Henry," another doctor said as he entered the hospital room, "How are you today?"

Henry was conscious, but not much more. He managed a

smile and determinedly replied, "OK, doc. And I'm going to be out of here in a few days." Henry's attitude remained cheerful and determined. And he got well.

"So what?" someone says. "He would have anyway."

But the team of physicians attending Henry stated, "If he had accepted the emotions of despair and defeat that his condition warranted, we are sure Henry would have died."

The scientific explanation for Henry's remarkable recovery is that good emotions (will, determination, and cheer) produced a maximum hormone balance in his body making up for what medicine alone could not do. I add a spiritual conclusion: Henry's courage-thoughts were God's healing power and love at work in his mind and body. Dr. William R. Parker, the psychologist who wrote *Prayer Can Change Your Life,* accurately described the phenomenon by saying, "What the deep mind desires, apparently the body will cooperate to do." [5]

Frank Manton discovered this truth. In his own words, he tells how he did it.

It was late afternoon. The house doctor had given me word that the surgeon would operate on me the next morning. A certain nervousness and fear came over me. I got out my daily devotional guide and Bible to read before trying to sleep. My attention was captured by this verse, "My presence shall go with you, and I will give you rest." That promise was to me as well as to Moses, in Exodus 33:14. Fear and nervousness fled.[6]

Inspirational Mind-Fillers

Fill your mind with inspiring thoughts and Bible verses when you sense fear approaching.

Every morning when you awake, go over some courage thoughts. For example: "I can do all things through Christ who strengthens me." "Today is the day the Lord has made." "I shall be happy and joyful today." "God loves me." "God forgives me." "God is good." "People, even my enemies, have good in them."

Every evening before you go to sleep, go over the good of the day. As you sleep, the good will percolate through your subconscious and influence your personality, thereby adding graciousness to your life.

When bad thoughts try to get in, immediately think good. War against negative, pessimistic, defeating thoughts, not with similar thinking, but with positive, peaceful, victorious thoughts.

Keep your thoughts on what you have to do. The prominent British Christian C. S. Lewis called this "the sense oughtness." Anchor your mind with what you must do and fear of things will disappear.

9. Faith-up your life and lose the power of your fears. "Come and follow me," Christ invites. "If they [you] follow me, the Father will honor them [you]" (John 12:26, LB). The faith is in a Christ who loves you, in the God who never loses and who has never made a loser out of anybody committed to him, and who looks out for you, who is honored to honor his believers, and who is the Great Provision for total human need.

Fears find more than their match in an open Christian instreamed by the Spirit of the Lord. That person is powered and motivated by One who is greater than any fear and any fear-source.

Fear	Faith
Fear-stricken person: Looks at a tough challenge and says, "It's too much."	Faith-stimulated person: Looks at a tough challenge and says, "God can—I will."
Fear-strangled person: Has a crisis and says, "I'm done for."	Faith-saturated person: Has a crisis and says, "I'll become a better person through this."

Fear-stripped person: Confronted by a problem and says, "There's no way out."

Faith-stirred person: Confronted by a problem and says, "Now what's the best way to handle this?"

It is certain that "God has not given us a spirit of fear, but a spirit of power and love and a sound mind" (2 Tim. 1:7, Phillips). That is your power promise. Apply it today and you will become an overcomer.

Notes

Chapter 1

1. Charles L. Wallis, ed., *A Treasury of Sermon Illustrations* (Nashville: Abingdon Press, Series AD), p. 99.
2. Harry Emerson Fosdick, *On Being a Real Person* (New York: Harper & Row, Publishers, 1942), p. 72.
3. Wallis, ed., *A Treasury*, p. 226.
4. James Stalker, *Imago Christi* (New York: A. C. Armstrong & Son, 1890), p. 138.
5. Fulton Oursler, *Modern Parables* (New York: Doubleday & Company, 1950), p. 88.

Chapter 2

1. Cecil Osborne, *The Art of Understanding Yourself* (Grand Rapids, Mich.: Zondervan Pub. House, 1967), p. 69.
2. David Schwarz, *The Magic of Thinking Big* (New York: Cornerstone Library, 1959), p. 7.
3. Charles Wallis, ed., *A Treasury of Sermon Illustrations* (Nashville: Abingdon Press, Series AD), p. 169.
4. Leslie Weatherhead, *Why Do Men Suffer?* (Nashville: Abingdon-Cokesbury Press, 1936), p. 214.
5. *The International Dictionary of Thoughts* (Chicago: J. G. Ferguson Pub. Co., 1969), p. 193.

Chapter 3

1. Frank C. Laubach, *Prayer Is the Mightiest Force in the World* (Old Tappan, N.J.: Fleming H. Revell Co., 1946), p. 193.
2. "Thought for the Day," *San Gabriel Valley* (Calif.) *Tribune,* 1969.
3. "International Copyright," *The Complete Poetical Works of James Russell Lowell,* Cambridge Edition, ed. by Horace E. Scudder (Boston: Houghton Mifflin, 1925), p. 433, used by permission.
4. Viktor E. Frankl, *Man's Search for Meaning* (New York: Washington Square Press, 1963), p. 179.
5. Rollo May, *The Art of Counseling* (Nashville: Abingdon-Cokesbury Press, 1938), p. 159.
6. George Matheson story from Walter B. Knight, *Knight's Treasury of Illustrations* (Grand Rapids, Mich.: Eerdman's Pub. Co., 1963), p. 375.
7. Leslie Weatherhead, *Why Do Men Suffer?* (Nashville: Abingdon-Cokesbury Press, 1936).
8. Frankl, *Man's Search for Meaning,* p. 206.

Chapter 4

1. Judson Gooding, "How to Cope With Boredom," *Reader's Digest,* September 1976, p. 51.
2. Charles L. Wallis, ed., *A Treasury of Sermon Illustrations* (Nashville: Abingdon Press, Series AD), p. 289.
3. "Key to Long Life? Enjoy Your Job," *San Gabriel Valley* (Calif.) *Tribune,* 25 December, 1972, p. 6A.
4. Wilfred Peterson, *The Art of Living* (New York: Simon & Schuster, 1960).

5. Dale Evans Rogers, *The Woman at the Well* (Old Tappan, N.J.: Fleming H. Revell Co., 1972), p. 237.
6. David Schwarz, *The Magic of Thinking Big* (New York: Cornerstone Library, 1959), p. 101.

Chapter 5

1. Reuel L. Howe, *Man's Need and God's Action* (New York: The Seabury Press, 1953), p. 15.
2. O. Hobart Mowrer, *The New Group Therapy* (Princeton, N.J.: D. Van Nostrand Co., 1964), p. 226.
3. Sidney S. Jourard, *The Transparent Self* (Princeton, N.J.: D. Van Nostrand Co., 1964), p. 26.
4. James R. Dolby, *I, Too, Am Man* (Waco, Texas: Word Books, 1969), p. 3.
5. Alex Thomas, "Hellbent for Success," *Faith/At/Work Magazine*, May–June, 1967, p. 3.

Chapter 6

1. Hugh Walpole, *Vanessa*, quoted in Charles L. Wallis, ed., *A Treasury of Sermon Illustrations* (Nashville: Abingdon Press, Series AD), p. 138.
2. Richard Crooks, "Singing Iceman," *The American Magazine*, April 1936, p. 114.

Chapter 7

1. Norman Vincent Peale, *Favorite Stories of Positive Faith* (Pawling, N.Y.: Foundation for Christian Living, 1975), p. 24.
2. Frances Gardner, *Hotline to Heaven* (N.Y.: Pyramid Books, 1971), p. 7.

Chapter 8

1. Alexis Carrel, *Reflections On Life* (N.Y.: Hawthorn Books, 1952).

Chapter 9

1. Walter B. Knight, *Knight's Treasury of Illustrations* (Grand Rapids, Mich.: Eerdman's Pub. Co., 1963), p. 64.

Chapter 10

1. Bruce Larson, *Dare to Live Now* (Grand Rapids, Mich.: Zondervan Pub. House, 1965), p. 78.
2. John Oxenham, "In Christ There Is No East or West," reprinted by permission of the American Tract Society, Oradell, New Jersey.
3. "Thought for the Day," *San Gabriel Valley* (Calif.) *Tribune*, 1971.
4. Maxwell Maltz, *Creative Living for Today* (New York: Pocket Books, 1970), p. 147.
5. William R. Parker, *Prayer Can Change Your Life* (Englewood Cliffs, N.J.: Prentice-Hall, 1957), p. 59.
6. Walter B. Knight, *Knight's Treasury of Illustrations* (Grand Rapids, Mich.: Eerdman's Pub. Co., 1963).